TEACHING LITERACY THROUGH THE ARTS

TOOLS FOR TEACHING LITERACY

Donna Ogle and Camille Blachowicz, Series Editors

This highly practical series includes two kinds of books: (1) grade-specific titles for first-time teachers or those teaching a particular grade for the first time; (2) books on key literacy topics that cut across all grades, such as integrated instruction, English language learning, and comprehension. Written by outstanding educators who know what works based on extensive classroom experience, each research-based volume features hands-on activities, reproducibles, and best practices for promoting student achievement.

TEACHING LITERACY IN SIXTH GRADE
Karen Wood and Maryann Mraz

TEACHING LITERACY IN KINDERGARTEN
Lea M. McGee and Lesley Mandel Morrow

INTEGRATING INSTRUCTION: LITERACY AND SCIENCE
Judy McKee and Donna Ogle

TEACHING LITERACY IN SECOND GRADE
Jeanne R. Paratore and Rachel L. McCormack

TEACHING LITERACY IN FIRST GRADE
Diane Lapp, James Flood, Kelly Moore, and Maria Nichols

PARTNERING FOR FLUENCY
Mary Kay Moskal and Camille Blachowicz

TEACHING LITERACY THROUGH THE ARTS
Nan L. McDonald and Douglas Fisher

TEACHING
LITERACY
through the Arts

Nan L. McDonald
Douglas Fisher

Series Editors' Note by Donna Ogle and Camille Blachowicz

THE GUILFORD PRESS
New York   London

KH

© 2006 The Guilford Press
A Division of Guilford Publications, Inc.
72 Spring Street, New York, NY 10012
www.guilford.com

Printed in the United States of America

This book is printed on acid-free paper.

Last digit is print number: 9 8 7 6 5 4 3 2 1

Library of Congress Cataloging-in-Publication Data

McDonald, Nan (Nan Leslie), 1950–
    Teaching literacy through the arts / Nan L. McDonald, Douglas Fisher.
       p. cm. —(Tools for teaching literacy)
    Includes bibliographical references and index.
    ISBN-10: 1-59385-280-0 ISBN-13: 978-1-59385-280-1 (pbk.)
    ISBN-10: 1-59385-281-9 ISBN-13: 978-1-59385-281-8 (cloth)
    1. Language arts (Elementary) 2. Arts—Study and teaching
(Elementary) 3. Interdisciplinary approach in education. I. Fisher,
Douglas, 1965– II. Title. III. Series.
    LB1576.M39745 2006
    372.6—dc22

                          2005031506

6/23/06

To our nieces and nephews,
Kasey Ring, Calvin Butz,
Dominique Smith, and Kaila Smith

ABOUT THE AUTHORS

Nan L. McDonald, EdD, is Associate Professor of Music Education at San Diego State University School of Music and Dance and also teaches integrated arts to teachers and students in K–12 classrooms. She is the author of numerous articles in music, arts, and literacy journals as well as a program author for the Scott Foresman/Silver Burdett Music K–8 music text series *Making Music*. Dr. McDonald is the Director of Integrated Arts for the City Heights Educational Collaborative and is the recipient of the 2000 Outstanding University Music Educator Award from the California Association for Music Education and the 2003 Outstanding Faculty Award from San Diego State University College of Professional Studies and Fine Arts.

Douglas Fisher, PhD, a former English teacher and language development specialist, is Professor of Language and Literacy Education at San Diego State University and the Director of Professional Development for the City Heights Educational Collaborative. He is the recipient of an International Reading Association Celebrate Literacy Award as well as a Christa McAuliffe Award for Excellence in Teacher Education. He has published numerous articles and books on reading and literacy, integrated arts, differentiated instruction, and curriculum design.

SERIES EDITORS' NOTE

This is an exciting time to be involved in literacy education. Across the United States, thoughtful practitioners and teacher educators are developing and fine-tuning their instructional practices to maximize learning opportunities for children. These cutting-edge practices deserve to be shared more broadly. Because of these changes, we have become aware of the need for a series of books for thoughtful practitioners who want a practical, research-based overview of current topics in literacy instruction. We also collaborate with staff developers and study group directors who want effective inservice materials that they can use with professionals and colleagues at many different levels that provide specific insights about literacy instruction. Thus the Tools for Teaching Literacy series was created.

This series is distinguished by having each volume written by outstanding educators who are noted for their knowledge and contributions to research, theory, and best practices in literacy education. They are also well-known staff developers who spend time in real classrooms working alongside teachers applying these insights. We think the series authors are unparalleled in these qualifications.

Active and engaged students learn more. In this volume, Nan L. McDonald and Douglas Fisher demonstrate clearly how teachers can involve students of all ages and enliven classrooms through integration of the arts with literacy learning. The wonderful examples show how each aspect of literacy development can be enhanced by the creative addition of music, drama, visual arts, and movement. The activities and extensive unit plans provide clear guidelines for how teachers can breathe life into the curriculum. The book is especially needed now in this era of accountability and test-consciousness. Once read, it will surely be shared widely!

DONNA OGLE
CAMILLE BLACHOWICZ

ACKNOWLEDGMENTS

The completion of this book would not have been possible without the support of Price Charities, San Diego State University, and the City Heights Educational Collaborative. Price Charities has consistently funded the arts and provided unprecedented access to arts instruction for public school children. Our students in music education and teacher education have allowed us to experiment with our ideas and have provided us with lesson feedback and reflections.

We have had the opportunity to learn alongside a group of dedicated educators at Rosa Parks Elementary, Monroe Clark Middle, and Hoover High schools. We have also been fortunate to work with a group of administrators who know that the arts can and should be used to complement and enhance literacy instruction. Dr. Ian Pumpian, Professor of Educational Leadership at San Diego State University, has supported the integration of the arts as a cornerstone of instructional renewal in urban schools. The City Heights K–16 integrated arts team and the literacy leadership team have consistently contributed new curricula and ideas for the students in City Heights.

We have also been fortunate to collaborate with content experts who have helped us identify ways to integrate the arts into their respective disciplines. Dr. Nancy Frey, Dr. Donna Ross, Dr. Donna Kopenski, and Dr. Emily Schell have engaged their curriculum teams in addressing the arts with literacy, science, math, and social studies, respectively.

Dr. Diane Lapp and Dr. James Flood encouraged us to write this book for the Tools for Teaching Literacy series. Their vision of language arts instruction guided us as we completed this project. We also would like to thank the series editors, Dr. Donna Ogle and Dr. Camille Blachowicz, for their feedback and support. And finally, we thank Chris Jennison and Craig Thomas of The Guilford Press for their expert editorial guidance.

Permission to reproduce covers from the following books has been granted by their publishers:

Joseph Had a Little Overcoat by Simms Taback, copyright 1999 by Simms Taback. Used by permission of Viking Penguin, A Division of Penguin Young Readers Group. A Member of Penguin Group (USA) Inc., 345 Hudson Street, New York, NY 10014. All rights reserved.

Lives of the Artists: Masterpieces, Messes (and What the Neighbors Thought) by Kathleen Krull, illustrations copyright 1994 by Kathryn Hewitt, reproduced by permission of Harcourt, Inc.

Sweet Clara and the Freedom Quilt by Deborah Hopkinson, paintings by James Ransome, copyright 1993 by Alfred Knopf, reproduced by permission of Alfred Knopf.

E is for Enchantment: A New Mexico Alphabet by Helen Foster James, illustrations by Neecy Twinem, copyright 2004, reproduced by permission of Sleeping Bear Press.

The Moon Book by Gail Gibbons, copyright 1998, reproduced by permission of Holiday House.

Mouse Paint by Ellen Stoll Walsh, copyright 1989 by Ellen Stoll Walsh, reprinted by permission of Harcourt, Inc.

Esperanza Rising by Pam Muñoz Ryan. Jacket illustration copyright 2000 by Joe Cepeda. Reprinted by permission of Scholastic, Inc.

Dangerous Planet by Bryn Barnard, copyright 2003 by Bryn Barnard. Used by permission of Crown Publishers, an imprint of Random House Children's Books, a division of Random House, Inc.

Fiesta Feminina by Mary-Joan Gerson, illustrations by Maya Christina Gonzalez, copyright 2001, reproduced by permission of Barefoot Books.

Martin's Big Words: The Life of Dr. Martin Luther King Jr. by Doreen Rappaport, illustrations by Bryan Collier, cover art by Flip Schulke, copyright 2001, reproduced by permission of Hyperion Books for Children.

Dem Bones by Bob Barner, copyright 1996, reproduced by permission of Chronicle Books.

Follow the Drinking Gourd by Jeanette Winter, copyright 1988, reproduced by permission of Alfred Knopf.

CONTENTS

TEACHING LITERACY THROUGH THE ARTS

CHAPTER 1

THE FIVE W'S OF INTEGRATED ARTS

In my classroom

. . . the arts bring voice and life to students' thoughts, emotions, and connections to their learning. This learning engages them in a multisensory way. It is a safe haven for self-expression.

—Carlie Ward, grade 5 teacher

CHAPTER 1 ANTICIPATION GUIDE

Before reading this chapter: A = agree D = disagree	Statements	After reading this chapter: A = agree D = disagree
	Teachers should attend to at least six kinds of art.	
	Students need access to arts specialists and integrated arts instruction.	
	Learning with and through the arts can be done at school, at home, and in the community.	
	The arts can be used to increase literacy achievement.	
	Arts instruction in the elementary and middle school classrooms should be optional.	

Many classroom teachers regularly incorporate arts activities (music, movement and dance, drama/theater, visual art) into their teaching. Those who do describe how their students become more interested and involved with the learning at hand, and by doing so, markedly increase literacy skills. These teachers also report that their students are more likely to remember the content they are learning because they are able to create and actively express the deeper meanings of that content through drawing, painting, movement, dramatization, singing, group projects, and more. *Simply put, learning with and through the arts enlivens instruction, increases student involvement, and deepens both the meaning and memory of the learning at hand.*

But what about the needs of classroom teachers who would like to integrate the arts into their classrooms to increase literacy development but may need some guidance, materials, and practical examples to get started? Good news! *The purpose of this guidebook is to provide K–8 teachers with information about teaching with and through the arts (e.g., music, drama/theater, visual arts, movement/dance) to enhance literacy instruction.* Through this guidebook, we hope you will gain a deeper understanding of how to teach with and through the arts to increase student literacy learning in your classroom. Let's get started.

This chapter provides an overview of integrated arts by answering five essential questions: what?, why?, who?, where?, and when? These questions and answers will provide you with information and resources about teaching and learning with and through the arts as you facilitate the literacy achievement of your students.

WHAT EXACTLY ARE THE FOUR ARTS?

We have written this book to communicate many practical ways teachers can and do teach with and through the arts. In order to make our way through these direct K–8 classroom examples, we may need first to take a brief look at the content of each of the four arts and what kinds of activities our students can do in each of the arts.

Music

Within musical contexts, students can learn to do many things. They can sing, play instruments, perform, improvise and compose music; read and notate music; listen to, analyze, describe, and evaluate music; and understand the relationships between music, the other arts, and disciplines outside the arts. They can also learn to understand music in relation to history and culture (Music Educators National Conference [MENC], 1994).

For a practical classroom-teacher-created list of specific activities students can do involving music connected to literacy instruction, see Table 1.1.

Visual Arts

Within the visual arts, our students learn about art through: understanding and applying media techniques and processes; using knowledge of structures and func-

TABLE 1.1. Activities Students Can Do in the Four Arts

Drama	Art	Music	Dance
Readers' Theatre	Found art	Songs	Movement response
Role playing	Painting	Instruments	Pantomime
Pantomime	Sketching	Chants/raps	Movement to poetry
Puppets	Crayons	Listening to music	Movement to ideas
Masks and characters	Papier-mâché	Poetry and music	Keeping a beat
Scriptwriting	Clay/sculpture	Rhythmic response	Movement to words
Finger plays	Scratch art	Found instruments	Games
Action to words	Photography	Composing	Moving with props
Scenery design	Textiles	History of music	Nonverbal communication
Lighting design	Artist study	Writing song lyrics	Body percussion
Sets and costumes	Torn paper art	Music of the world	Dances of the world
Tableaux of scenes	Mosaics	Symbols of music	Dances of differences eras
Creative drama games	Pastels/chalk	Reading music	Popular dances
	Charcoal	Study composers	Created dances
	Water color	Styles of music	Gestures—no words
	Pottery	Science of sound	Movement tableaux
	Crafts	Environmental sounds	
	Jewelry	Sound effects	
	Tie-dye	Music and mood	
	Print making	Musical theater	
	Stamp art	Performing music	
	Vegetable stamps	Writing about music	
	Murals	Writing about musicians	
	Stencil art		
	Fashion		
	History of art		
	Art of many cultures		
	Computer art		
	Writing about art		
	Studying artists' styles, lives		
	Science of color		
	Dioramas		

tions; choosing and evaluating a range of subject matter, symbols, and ideas; understanding the visual arts in relation to history and cultures; reflecting upon and assessing the characteristics of their work and the work of others; and making connections between the visual arts and other disciplines (MENC, 1994).

For a practical classroom-teacher-created list of specific activities students can do involving visual art connected to literacy instruction, see Table 1.1.

Theater and Drama

Within the contexts of the art of theater, our students learn in a variety of ways: scriptwriting and recording improvisations based on personal experiences, heritage, imagination, literature, and history; acting by assuming roles and interacting in improvisations; designing by visualizing and arranging environments for classroom dramatizations; directing by planning classroom dramatizations; researching by finding information to support classroom dramatizations; comparing and connecting art forms by describing theater and dramatic media (such as film, television, and electronic media); analyzing and explaining personal preferences and constructing meanings from classroom dramatizations and from theater, film, television, and electronic media productions; and understanding context by recognizing the role of theater, film, television, and electronic media in daily life (MENC, 1994).

For a practical classroom-teacher-created list of specific activities students can do involving theater connected to literacy instruction, see Table 1.1.

Dance and Movement

Through the art of dance, students can learn the following: demonstrating movement elements and skills as they perform dance; understanding choreography; understanding dance as a way to create and communicate meaning; applying and demonstrating critical and creative thinking skills in dance; demonstrating and understanding dance in various cultures and historical periods; making connections between dance and healthful living; and making connections between dance and other disciplines (MENC, 1994).

For a practical classroom-teacher-created list of specific activities students can do involving dance connected to literacy instruction, see Table 1.1.

WHAT DOES IT MEAN TO INFUSE LITERACY INSTRUCTION WITH AND THROUGH THE ARTS?

We believe that *all* children need instruction in the arts. In addition to learning about specific art forms and disciplines (music, dance, theater, and visual arts), students need actually to create and "do" the arts on a regular and ongoing basis. In addition, the arts provide powerful avenues for learning and developing literacy skills in the general classroom. In other words, arts education for all children is important unto itself (discipline specific) as well as *in connection to or infused into literacy contexts.* This type of arts integration is referred to in this book as *literacy through the arts.*

We believe *all* children need both specialized, sequential instruction in the arts (taught by arts specialists) *and* arts activities and experiences infused into their literacy instruction in the general classroom. This is a lofty expectation because we know that not all children have regular opportunities to experience specialized arts instruction (in all four arts) in kindergarten through grade 8. Furthermore, we know that while many classroom teachers have an appreciation for the arts, many do not feel they have the time, background, materials, or skills they need to infuse arts activities into their classroom literacy instruction. Many teachers may need guidance and support to begin rethinking and augmenting current teaching practices to include the powerful avenues for learning the arts can and do provide.

Simply put, we may need to rethink and discover new ways for teachers to begin to use the arts within literacy instruction. In the subsequent chapters of this book, you will be provided with many examples of how K–8 classroom teachers have utilized various arts activities to augment and enhance literacy instruction in phonics and phonemic awareness, vocabulary, fluency in reading and writing, comprehension, oral language, and background and prior knowledge. Through these many examples, we will explore how real teachers have purposely and successfully used arts activities to extend their students' literacy development.

WHY SHOULD I TEACH LITERACY WITH AND THROUGH THE ARTS?

The arts make all kinds of learning exciting. We know that the more involved students are, the more they learn. The making and doing of the arts can also

uniquely stimulate the senses and provide direct, active pathways to perceptions about the world around us. The arts provide a wealth of experience related to forms of human expression found in language as well as various forms of nonverbal and sensory communications such as gesture, emotions, feelings, sound, symbols, movement, shapes, colors, patterns, and designs (Gardner, 1984, 1993a, 1993b). Dance, theater, music, and the visual arts often communicate within nonverbal avenues of expression and use symbols that are simply not translatable to human language. By doing so, they provide important ways of knowing as essential forms of human discourse and inquiry (Eisner, 1980). Human language alone may not provide the sufficient means to communicate many life experiences, emotions and meanings (California Department of Education, 1996). (McDonald & Fisher, 2002, p. 4)

The following list provides some further reasons to include the arts within literacy instruction:

➢ *The arts enhance and motivate other learning* by utilizing systems that include students' "integrated sensory, attentional, cognitive, emotional, and motor capacities and are, in fact the driving forces behind all other learning" (Jensen, 2001, p. 2).

➢ *All students can benefit from arts activity*, including students who are marginalized or underserved, at-risk, and children with special needs. Students who receive learning opportunities with the arts benefit from better communication skills, friendships with others, and fewer instances of violence, racism, and other troubling and nonproductive behaviors (Fiske, 1999).

➢ *The arts increase literacy skills* in that students read, write, speak, and listen as they participate in the arts. They also encourage new types of literacy to emerge (Armstrong, 2003).

➢ *Students learn by doing and creating.* Engagement and attention are key to learning (Marzano, 2004). Hands-on and minds-on activities with and through the arts allow students to explore content in new ways.

➢ *Our students need to connect and exercise their literacy skills throughout their school day.* We know that literacy development can and does occur throughout the curriculum. Rather than thinking of literacy instruction as "something we've got to do every morning," we want our students to use their reading and writing skills within multiple and meaningful contexts throughout their day. The arts help provide those contexts and connections. If we begin to use arts activity to increase students' literacy skills, we can also naturally design opportunities for students to connect this learning in social studies, math, and science (Jacobs, 1989, 1997).

➢ *Arts activity linked to literacy instruction can provide students needed cultural relevance* through connections to various cultures and times and their unique contribution of visual art, music, theater, and dance.

➢ *The arts affect creativity and increase satisfaction.* Classroom teachers consistently report that they and their students are happiest and most productive during literacy instruction when engaged in creative ways of learning that the arts naturally provide. Many teachers also report that these are the most meaningful and memorable literacy learning experiences for their students.

WHO CAN TEACH LITERACY WITH AND THROUGH THE ARTS?

We believe that *all* K–8 classroom teachers can learn effective ways to incorporate the arts into their everyday literacy instruction. We consistently observe and hear from teachers on a daily basis and have included many of their ideas in this book. While we know that this kind of arts infusion into literacy instruction does not in any way replace the need for all students to have regular, specialized instruction in the arts taught by arts specialists, we know that arts activities can provide new and exciting ways for students actively to use and increase their literacy skills.

➢ *In order to make these changes, K–8 classroom teachers deserve opportunities to reflect and rethink their current literacy instruction.* Ask for time for these kinds of discussions at grade level, faculty meetings, and teacher resource/professional development days.

➢ *You may need to find one or more teaching peers who are interested in using the arts in their classroom.* Team your efforts. Get together and plan simple ways to incorporate some of the ideas presented in this book.

➢ *Talk to your teaching peers and listen to what they may already be doing in their own classrooms.* Find out what resources you already have at your school site to begin to develop some arts activities with a focus on literacy.

➢ *Ask your arts specialists and/or coordinators about ideas and resources for connecting literacy instruction to arts activities.* Ask them if they could share resources and even teach you activities to get started with these learning connections. Request that workshops on this topic be a part of professional growth days.

➢ *Finally, and ultimately, it is up to you*—one teacher—to be willing to experiment with new ways to improve literacy instruction for you and your students. You and your students have nothing to lose and quite a bit to gain!

WHERE CAN THIS TEACHING AND LEARNING TAKE PLACE?

Consider the possibility that your classroom is a *starting place* for learning through the arts. We know that students learn both in and beyond our classroom walls. If we are to experiment with exciting ways to connect arts activities to literacy instruction, we may need to explore some of the following:

➢ *Home.* This may include potential contributions and expertise volunteered by parents, grandparents, or other family members. Perhaps a checklist could be sent home to find out what talents and resources others can lend to arts activities in your classroom (visual art skills, crafts, storytelling, photography, singing or playing instruments, dance leadership, etc.). You might also suggest a list of things parents can do with their children, such as making art together, attending local arts events, reading books, and watching videos.

➢ *Community.* How long has it been since you have explored all your local museums, historical societies, community landmarks, and cultural centers? Go online, write or call, or better yet, visit local arts agencies (e.g., museums, young audiences, symphonies, theaters, dance studios, art studios and exhibits) and ask for information about programs of interest to teachers and students, artists-in-residence for your school, docent tours at museums, field trips, and visitors to your school.

➢ *Local universities, community colleges, and high schools* may be a source of potential activities of interest to you and your students (art shows, musicals, plays, and musical and dance concerts). All these arts events offer potential for students to learn about the arts and exercise their writing and reading abilities before and after the event. Often, high school and university-level arts productions will have reduced group rates and some free or inexpensive opportunities for K–8 students and teachers to attend. Call or e-mail the art, theater, music and dance departments at nearby high schools, colleges, and universities and ask to be sent their schedule of performances. Also ask if their students perform in schools and if they host any workshops for teachers in the arts. Sign up for a class!

➢ *Go online and investigate arts-education-related websites* appropriate for classroom teachers and students. You will be amazed at the possibilities for lesson ideas, resources, and materials.

➢ *Exchanges with other teachers and schoolwide projects.* Find every opportunity to have your students attend other classroom displays and informal performances of arts connected to literacy. Create a theme-based, schoolwide focus on poetry or children's literature themes (e.g., friendship) in which various classroom teachers can contribute student artwork, music, dances, and dramatic presentations connected to literacy. Be sure your principal and others know of your efforts!

➢ *Create a curriculum team of peers.* Find two or three other classroom teachers in your grade level and beyond who are interested in arts in literacy instruction.

Brainstorm ways to include home, community, higher education, parents, students, and other teachers. Make a commitment to share ideas and visit each other's classrooms. Let others know what you are doing. Be willing to create and experiment together.

WHEN CAN I FIND TIME TO TEACH WITH AND THROUGH THE ARTS?

We know that our students learn best by doing and creating, so shouldn't one priority be to incorporate arts activities into our classroom literacy instruction regularly? This book will provide a vast variety of examples of how other K–8 classroom teachers have used the arts. Some, if not many, of these lessons may appeal to you personally and seem doable in your own classroom. As you read through the lesson examples, you might jot down ideas on Post-it notes and attach them to the lesson example. Make notes to yourself of how this type of lesson activity could be incorporated into one of your own units of study. Decide on two or three ideas and make a commitment to try an idea once per week. Then, once you have experimented with a few ideas, try creating your own and use them as often as you can.

HOW DO I GET STARTED?

You have already begun! Congratulations!

Change in how we teach comes slowly and involves considerable courage, discipline, experimentation, and reflection. You should know that the classroom teacher/contributors to this book started with little or no prior knowledge of how to teach with and through the arts. Know that their original lesson ideas were developed through frequent experimentation with their own and others' ideas. Allow yourself to learn from their courageous and innovative spirits.

The following section will outline all you need to know to make your way through the remaining chapters of this book. In later chapters, you will read many examples in which music, visual arts, theater and drama, and dance and movement activities were connected to literacy instruction involving the following: oral language, concepts of print, a sense of story and sequence, phonics and phonemic awareness, background knowledge and vocabulary, fluency, comprehension, and writing. Allow these lesson examples to serve as food for thought. These teacher contributors continue to use the arts whenever they can as they have discovered (as you will) that the benefits of these activities far exceed the sacrifice of time involved to plan and teach them. Start simply and watch your efforts grow. Then congratulate yourself and your students for all creative efforts!

HOW TO USE THIS BOOK

Remember, the purpose of this book is to provide you with information about *teaching with and through the arts to enhance literacy instruction*. With that clear purpose in mind, we have included three key features in this book. First, as you read this book you will find out a lot about the various components of literacy instruction necessary for students to learn to speak, listen, read, write, and think. Second, you will explore the four arts described in Chapter 1 in great detail. And finally, you will find complete thematic units that integrate the content areas (social studies, science, language arts, and math) and the various arts (music, visual arts, drama, and dance) to produce learning opportunities for students. Let's consider each of these three key features in a bit more detail.

Learning with and through the Arts
Linked with Literacy Components

Every teacher is concerned with his or her students' literacy development because literacy skills are foundational to everything we learn and know. We all read, write, speak, listen, and observe to obtain and share information. Stated another way, all learning is language-based. Thus, children must be taught how to read, write, speak, listen, and view *and* how to use these literacy skills in other content areas.

Literacy researchers have identified a number of components that are required to ensure that all students become literate. These components are organized into three main areas: oral language, reading, and writing.

Oral Language

Often considered the most basic literacy skills, listening and speaking are the base from which we build students' reading, writing, and thinking. Over time, young children move from babbling and cooing to saying individual words to combining words in sentences to speaking in front of their peers. The interaction between speaking and listening should be fairly obvious, so suffice it to say that classroom time should be devoted to these skills on a regular basis.

As you may have guessed, not all talk is equal. Students need to have opportunities to talk about things that matter and to talk about academic topics. Just chatting with a friend may be enjoyable and may provide for practice but it does not ensure that students become increasingly sophisticated communicators. Students need to learn to share their complex thinking, to listen to their peers and evaluate what they say, to make their arguments well, and to consider the perspectives of others (e.g., Roser & Martinez, 1995; Smith, 2001; Staab, 1992). As you will read in this book, the arts can facilitate students' oral language development.

Reading

In the past decade a significant amount of attention has been paid to reading development. Over the years, consensus has been reached regarding the components of reading development that are critical to students' learning. These include phonemic awareness, phonics, reading fluency, vocabulary development, and reading comprehension. A discussion of each of these critical components can be found in Figure 1.1.

In addition to these components, we have added the idea of building background knowledge. We know, for example, that students learn new information more effectively when they already know something about the topic. We also know that students learn new information more effectively when concepts in that area mean something to them, either because of their personal experiences and background or because they have been taught something about this in the past (Harmin, 1994; Marzano, 2004). Our focus on reading development includes the concept of building background knowledge.

Writing

To date, there has been much less consensus on writing development. In addition, writing instruction has been somewhat neglected with the significant push for reading achievement. Having said that, we know that writing matters and that students must be taught to write well.

From research on good writers (e.g., Spandel, 2004), we know that there are at least six traits, plus the presentation of the writing, that we can use to organize writing instruction (see 6 + 1 writing traits at www.nwrel.org):

1. *Ideas*, the heart of the message.
2. *Organization*, the internal structure of the piece.
3. *Voice*, the personal tone and flavor of the author's message.
4. *Word Choice*, the vocabulary a writer chooses to convey meaning.
5. *Sentence fluency*, the rhythm and flow of the language.

Reading with children and helping them practice specific reading components can dramatically improve their ability to read. Scientific research shows that there are five essential components of reading that children must be taught in order to learn to read. Adults can help children learn to be good readers by systematically practicing these five components:

- Recognizing and using individual sounds to create words, or **phonemic awareness**. Children need to be taught to hear sounds in words and that words are made up of the smallest parts of sound, or phonemes.
- Understanding the relationships between written letters and spoken sounds, or **phonics**. Children need to be taught the sounds individual printed letters and groups of letters make. Knowing the relationships between letters and sounds helps children to recognize familiar words accurately and automatically, and "decode" new words.
- Developing the ability to read a text accurately and quickly, or **reading fluency**. Children must learn to read words rapidly and accurately in order to understand what is read. When fluent readers read silently, they recognize words automatically. When fluent readers read aloud, they read effortlessly and with expression. Readers who are weak in fluency read slowly, word by word, focusing on decoding words instead of comprehending meaning.
- Learning the meaning and pronunciation of words, or **vocabulary development**. Children need to actively build and expand their knowledge of written and spoken words, what they mean and how they are used.
- Acquiring strategies to understand, remember and communicate what is read, or **reading comprehension strategies**. Children need to be taught comprehension strategies, or the steps good readers use to make sure they understand text. Students who are in control of their own reading comprehension become purposeful, active readers.

FIGURE 1.1. Five essential components of reading. From U.S. Department of Education (2003).

6. *Conventions*, the mechanical correctness.

+1 *Presentation*, how the writing actually looks on the page.

The arts allow students to develop their writing and to receive feedback as they write. In addition, with the arts, students write for authentic purposes and audiences, which in turn motivates them to write.

It is important to note that this book is not a reading or writing methods book. There are a number of great books on teaching children to become literate (see Figure 1.2 for a list of good choices). This book focuses on the role that music, visual arts, theater and drama, and dance and movement can play in the overall literacy achievement of students in grades K–8.

Focused on Each of the Four Arts

Chapters 2, 3, 4, and 5 discuss music, visual art, theater and drama, and dance and movement. These chapters explore how activities using those arts contribute to literacy. In each of these chapters, you will read about real K–8 classroom teachers and their students and what happened when literacy instruction was infused with arts activities. For more information on the visual and performing arts standards that guide our profession, see your state department of education website or the Music Educators National Conference (www.menc.org) for their joint position statement on content standards relative to the arts.

Complete Examples of Thematic Units and Resources

While you are reading Chapters 2–5, you will be referred to Appendices A–F. These appendices are integrated instructional units in which arts activities are featured in combination with literacy. Each appendix includes rationale, detailed teaching sequences, extensive resource lists, assessments, ideas for performance sharing, and more.

➤ *Appendix A.* "Stormy Weather: Leading Purposeful Curriculum Integration with and through the Arts" is an integrated unit surrounding the science theme of changing weather. Students view art about weather patterns, make art projects, sing, dance, recite chants, and participate in a delightful shared performance (narration provided): A CNN-type weathercast peppered with performances and sharing of their weather-themed arts activities.

➤ *Appendix B.* "Movin' Along: The Poetry of Transportation" (primary grades). Within this creative third-grade general classroom model, poetry about trains continues into integrated activities using music and movement, musical listening, discussion, art, and creative writing projects designed for active student

Fearn, L., & Farnan, N. (2000). *Interactions: Teaching writing and the language arts.* Boston: Houghton Mifflin.

Fisher, D., & Frey, N. (2004). *Improving adolescent literacy: Strategies at work.* Upper Saddle River, NJ: Merrill Prentice Hall.

Frey, N., & Fisher, D. (2005). *Language arts workshop: Purposeful reading and writing instruction.* Upper Saddle River, NJ: Merrill Prentice Hall.

Lapp, D., Flood, J., Brock, C., & Fisher, D. (2006). *Teaching reading to every child* (4th ed.). Mahwah, NJ: Erlbaum.

FIGURE 1.2. Resources for teaching reading and writing.

involvement and expression of sensory meanings of the words and thematic content. Performance sharing ideas are suggested as well as resources for poetry and children's literature about transportation, songs, musical listening samples, and teacher resources for integrative, thematic teaching.

➤ *Appendix C.* "Expressive Literacy with in Musical Listening: *The Moldau*, a Symphonic Poem by Smetana" (upper elementary and middle school) is a teaching model of a music listening lesson for third- through sixth-grade students and future classroom teachers (nonspecialists). The unit was designed to help educators stimulate student interest, literacy skills, and heightened involvement in listening to an 11-minute symphonic poem (orchestral), *The Moldau* by Bedrich Smetana (1824–1884). Introductory group dramatic choral readings and art illustration were integrated within musical listening activity.

➤ *Appendix D.* "Haiku: Active Learning with and through the Arts" (upper elementary and middle school) is a unit taught to third- through fifth-grade students as well as practicing classroom and future elementary teachers. In it, resources and teaching sequences are offered surrounding the study of Japanese haiku poetry, culture, artists, and poets. Children's literature is a centerpiece of this curriculum unit as students and teachers actively learn about the life and times of the haiku master Basho (1763–1827). Students then form cooperative, project-based learning groups to create movement, visual art, and expressive speech (theater), as they learn about traditional Japanese music and art. Traditional haiku poetry comes alive as an integrated arts performance piece tied to literacy and oral language development.

➤ *Appendix E.* "American Panoramas: A Literature-Based Integrated Arts Curriculum Unit" (elementary and middle school) suggests ways in which elementary and middle school classroom informational texts (social studies, science) can be easily supplemented with quality children's literature, songs, poems, creative movement, and visual art about the American terrain. This integrated arts unit pairs children's literature and poetry about terrain with active reader response through music, dance, theater, and visual art; ways to create group projects and cooperative learning opportunities for students through integrated arts activities; suggestions for exhibition and performance of student works tied to this theme; and extensive resource lists for general classroom use.

➤ *Appendix F.* "Jazz Listening Activities: Children's Literature and Authentic Music Samples" (upper elementary and middle school) offers a curriculum unit model and suggestions for teachers to create active introductory listening lessons for upper elementary and middle school students paired with biographies (children's literature) about jazz and jazz artists. The authentic listening samples appear within an annotated discography correlated to the content and sequence of specific children's literature sources about jazz. This model curriculum is designed to introduce the young reader to the sound of jazz, jazz musicians, and the historical and cultural contexts in which this art form was and continues to be actively created. The activities presented focus on active assessments and include the following: reading, listening checklists, analysis, discussion, journal writing, visual art projects, and cooperative group work toward student performance projects to include music, drama, and visual art.

Important Tips for Using the Book

This book is meant to be read in sequential order, as ideas and discussions often build upon previously discussed material. Always take a moment and fill in the Anticipation Guide before and immediately after reading each chapter. While the above six appendices' units take a little more time to read than the shorter classroom examples imbedded within each chapter's discussion, we would like to suggest that you read each appendix as it is mentioned. We have referred you to these appendices because we believe teaching with and through the arts is more comprehensively understood within the broader context of a complete instructional unit. Finally, be sure to consider and discuss the various study questions and suggested activities mentioned at the end of each chapter. By doing so, you will further develop your own skills in creating arts activities linked to literacy instruction.

Let's get started! Now, what about music?

STUDY QUESTIONS AND ACTIVITIES

1. Experience each of the four arts in your community over the next few weeks.
2. Explain to a teaching colleague why integrated arts instruction matters and consider this person's response.
3. Make a list of ways you could address the four arts within your classroom. Discuss your list with someone else.
4. Talk to two or more teachers or student teachers at your school site and find out/ discuss the following information:
   - What supplies, room space, and equipment, is there at your school that could be used for arts activities in your classroom? Make a list. Don't forget to check the school library for music textbooks and recordings, Readers' Theatre, art books and project instructions, plays, etc.
   - What are the arts interests of these other teachers? At your grade level

and beyond, who feels most comfortable in leading songs? movement? drama and theater? visual art?
- Who is your district coordinator or resource teacher in charge of the arts?
- Is there a media center for your district? If so, what materials are there for teaching with and through the arts?

REFERENCES

Armstrong, T. (2003). *The multiple intelligences of reading and writing: Making the words come alive.* Alexandria, VA: Association for Supervision and Curriculum Development.

California Department of Education. (1996). *Visual and performing arts framework for California public schools: Kindergarten through grade twelve.* Sacramento, CA: Author.

Eisner, E. (1980). The arts as a way of knowing. *Principal, 60*(1), 11–14.

Fiske, E. (Ed.) (1999). *Champions of change: The impact of the arts on learning.* Washington, DC: The Arts Education Partnership and the President's Committee on the Arts and the Humanities. [Available from www.artsedge.kennnedy-center.org/champions]

Gardner, H. (1984). *A cognitive approach to creativity.* New York: Basic Books.

Gardner, H. (1993a). *Frames of mind: The theory of multiple intelligences* (Tenth Anniversary Edition). New York: Basic Books.

Gardner, H. (1993b). *Multiple intelligences: The theory in practice.* New York: Basic Books.

Harmin, M. (1994). *Inspiring active learning: A handbook for teachers.* Alexandria, VA: Association for Supervision and Curriculum Development.

Jacobs, H. H. (1989). *Interdisciplinary curriculum: Design and implementation.* Alexandria, VA: Association for Supervision and Curriculum Development.

Jacobs, H. H. (1997). *Mapping the big picture: Integrating curriculum and assessment K–12.* Alexandria, VA: Association for Supervision and Curriculum Development.

Jensen, E. (2001). *Arts with the brain in mind.* Alexandria, VA: Association for Supervision and Curriculum Development.

Marzano, R. J. (2004). *Building background knowledge for academic achievement: Research on what works in schools.* Alexandria, VA: Association for Supervision and Curriculum Development.

McDonald, N., & Fisher, D. (2002). *Developing arts-loving readers: Top 10 questions teachers are asking about integrated arts education.* Lanham, MD: Scarecrow.

Music Educators National Conference. (1994). Dance, music, theatre, visual arts: What every young American should know and be able to do in the arts: National standards for arts education. Reston, VA: Author.

Roser, N. L., & Martinez, M. G. (Eds.). (1995). *Book talk and beyond: Children and teachers respond to literature.* Newark, DE: International Reading Association.

Smith, P. G. (Ed.). (2001). *Talking classrooms: Shaping children's learning through oral language instruction*. Newark, DE: International Reading Association.

Spandel, V. (2004). *Creating writers through 6-trait writing assessment and instruction* (4th ed.). Boston: Allyn & Bacon.

Staab, C. (1992). *Oral language for today's classroom*. Markham, Ontario: Pippin.

U.S. Department of Education, Office of Intergovernmental and Interagency Affairs, Educational Partnerships and Family Involvement Unit. (2003). *Reading tips for parents*. Washington, DC: Author.

THE ROLE OF MUSIC IN LITERACY ACHIEVEMENT

In my classroom . . .

. . . we participate in the arts constantly. Music is a wonderful way to get students excited about the content they're learning and to help them comprehend the content. We also use movement in conjunction with poetry to help students excel in oral language and vocabulary. I discovered that when my students are doing visual art like drawing to represent their learning, they are much more enthusiastic and excited about subjects like social studies. My students also love to dance. I see so much happiness and unity when they are dancing.

—Adrienne Feistel

. . . my students light up when we sing an old song that they have already learned. There is a confidence they show because they have learned that song and sing it with ease. They make connections between songs and other songs or stories just like we ask them to make connections with literature texts. A similar joyful confidence comes out when they take part in an old dance that they have learned. The arts help them feel energized about learning and accomplished by new skills.

—Mary Flood

. . . my students eagerly anticipate the performance of their classmates on a poem/song at the end of a unit. The happiness I see on their faces encourages me to make time for the arts. The experiences the arts create will never be forgotten.

—Pam Pham-Barron

CHAPTER 2 ANTICIPATION GUIDE

Before reading this chapter: A = agree D = disagree	Statements	After reading this chapter: A = agree D = disagree
	Incorporating musical activity into my literacy instruction takes too much time.	
	The use of music during literacy instruction requires teacher talent.	
	There are natural links between classroom musical activity and important instructional goals in literacy development.	
	A child's personal confidence in learning language can be increased by participation in singing.	
	Song texts and singing are the only musical activities linked to literacy development.	

Across the world, teachers are working to improve the literacy performance of their students. Many teachers have created and implemented innovative approaches to translate current research into classroom practices. Given the explosion of information available about literacy development, teachers are considering new approaches to their instructional repertoires. For example, we know that young children's developing literacy skills are exercised when "emergent readers hear, sing, discuss, play with, and write songs because "they are building important background knowledge that they will draw upon during later reading and writing experiences. With each new song, students learn concepts and word meanings that they will encounter in print" (Smith, 2000, p. 647).

The intent of this chapter is to identify and define literacy instructional goals with specific examples of musical activities that foster language and literacy development. We begin with a conversation about oral language development. We then move to a discussion of reading and writing development. We focus the discussion on concepts of print and the understanding of story structures, phonemic awareness and phonics, background knowledge and vocabulary, fluency, comprehension, and writing activities. For each of the following literacy concepts, musical examples are provided, shared by teachers whom we have been privileged to observe.

ORAL LANGUAGE DEVELOPMENT

Oral language—both speaking and listening—is considered the precursor to print literacy. Helping students learn to share their ideas orally and listen carefully is critical in today's world. Having said that, it is important to note that oral-language-developed instruction should not stop when students begin to read and write. Throughout the grades, students need to increase their listening and speaking skills to the point that they can listen critically and evaluate information, share their ideas with large audiences, and vary their speech based on the audience at hand.

Students actively use oral language, of course, every time they sing the words to a song. Furthermore, a child's personal confidence in using language is increased by his or her participation in the overall sound of group singing. Shy students will participate without the fear of being singled out. Much learning transpires as new words are learned and used through speaking and singing.

In the processes of learning words to songs (or poetry), students are constantly repeating words in both spoken and sung contexts. They may be reading and rereading the words aloud from charts, overheads, song sheets, and so on. Also, they may be experimenting with different ways to say and/or sing those words using various voice inflections, loud and soft, fast and slow, emphasized words, and other expressive techniques involved in successful communication through oral language.

One example of creative opportunities for oral language skill development can be found within Appendix D. Using recorded music background, students are asked to experiment with different ways to "make the haiku come alive" by using highly expressive, musical/dramatic speech that "varies the tempo (speed) and dynamics (softs and louds) according to the feeling and meaning of the haiku" (McDonald, 2004, p. 20). The students are asked to work in cooperative groups and discuss how to perform their haiku selection using expressive speech and movement. In order to do this, they must discuss and repeat their haiku many times, experiment with ways to say it and move, and make decisions and coordinate their "performance" with others.

The student's use of oral language is not limited to performance of songs and poetry. Other learning events can elicit a great deal of talk and discussion from students. In the unit described in Appendix F, upper elementary and middle school students are introduced to jazz by being shown pictures of instruments as they listen to jazz recordings or by viewing short video clips of various jazz performers. The students are then engaged in a preliminary class discussion to discover what they may already know about jazz and its performers, origins, etc.: What is jazz? Who plays jazz? Where did jazz come from? How old is jazz? Is jazz heard today? Where? From this student discussion, a list of words is collected to describe jazz. Later, in that same unit, students participate in various oral group presentations about what they have learned about jazz. One event is "Meet Our Artist," where a group member plays the role of a famous jazz musician and tells stories about his or her life and experiences making music. The class is then invited to ask the "jazz artist" questions about his or her life and music.

CONCEPTS OF PRINT

One of the early predictors of reading success for young children is their understanding of the ways in which print functions. This construct, known as "concepts of print" (e.g., Clay, 1985) includes the knowledge that print, not pictures, contains the message, how to hold a book, the difference between upper- and lowercase letters, left-to-right print orientation, top-to-bottom directionality, and the use of punctuation marks.

Music is an excellent way to explore concepts of print. For example, when teachers use published music Big Books, large chart paper with chants or poetry written on them, they physically point to and model the left-to-right, top-to-bottom orientation and directionality that characterizes the English language. Similarly, as music teachers encourage students to follow along with the song text in their music books, students simultaneously hear the words and see them on paper. As students listen and sing, they begin to realize that the print contains meaning and that there are similarities between the print and the meaning.

In many instances, a teacher will incorporate the use of creative movement with singing to reinforce concepts of print. For example, we observed a teacher leading a folk song, "Hawaiian Rainbows." As the children slowly read aloud each line of the song text in rhythm (by pointing to that text in their songbooks), the teacher asked them for their ideas for simple arm movements to go with each line of the text. As the children carefully reread the words to the song, they determined there were four lines of text, needing four different creative movements. Many children also noticed the rhyming words at the end of each phrase (by/sky and me/sea).

> Hawaiian rainbows, white clouds roll by;
> You show your colors against the sky.
> Hawaiian rainbows, it seems to me,
> Reach from the mountain down to the sea.

The teacher then taught the song's melody (line by line in echo fashion) and added the children's movement ideas. At the end of this lesson, the children demonstrated their ability appropriately to master concepts of print within the active and expressive contexts of music and movement. Additionally, their total body involvement in the song's melody and movement served to heighten their understanding and enjoyment of the text.

A SENSE OF STORY AND SEQUENCE

Another important task for early readers to discern is the sense of story and sequence contained in narrative texts (e.g., Templeton, 1995). The earliest stories that children are likely to encounter are oral traditions and read-alouds. Understanding how stories work in terms of their structure "provides an inner model of the rhythms and patterns of written language" (Yaden, Smolkin, & Conlon, 1989, p. 208). As children begin to master the sense of story, more complex series of events are introduced. For example, classroom teachers use books to build students' understanding of story structures. A kindergarten teacher may start with *The Napping House* by Audrey Wood (1984) to create sense of sequence, then *Drummer Hoff* by Barbara Emberly (1987) and *Possum Come a-Knockin'* by Nancy Van Laan (1990).

Additionally, teachers can use some of the following examples of song/chant lyrics published as storybooks, including the following:

> *There Was an Old Lady Who Swallowed a Fly*, illustrated by Pam Adams (Child's Play International, 1999)
> *There Was an Old Lady Who Swallowed a Fly*, illustrated by Simms Taback (Viking, 1997)
> *Peanut Butter and Jelly*, illustrated by Nadine Bernard Westcott (Dutton, 1987)
> *The Wheels on the Bus* adapted and illustrated by Paul Zelinsky (Dutton, 1990)
> *Little Rabbit Foo Foo* by Michael Rosen (Aladdin, 1993)

Music contributes to students' understanding of stories and sequence. Each song that students learn has a story to tell, and teachers who integrate their curriculum enjoy building on this knowledge. In addition, several songs specifically address sequences. One teacher was observed leading the song "I Had an Old Coat," whose text tells the story of a ragged old coat that gradually wears out and is made smaller and smaller into a jacket, a shirt, a vest, a tie, a patch, and a button. Finally, when nothing is left of the old coat, the singer simply makes up a song!

As this teacher introduced the song's story sequence, she gave each child a piece of paper with a drawing of an old coat in the center of the page (see Figure 2.1). The old coat illustration was surrounded by a border of labeled drawings of the other story components of the song text (jacket, button, etc.). The children in

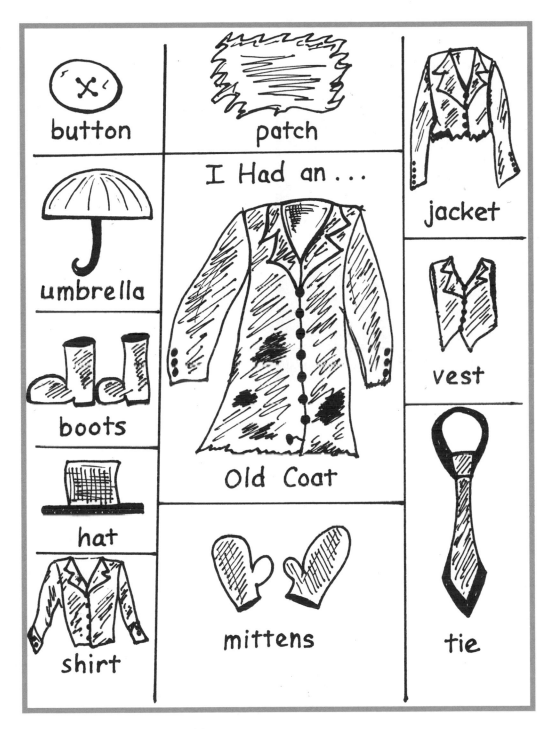

FIGURE 2.1. "I Had an Old Coat" activity.

From *Teaching Literacy through the Arts* by Nan L. McDonald and Douglas Fisher. Copyright 2006 by The Guilford Press. Permission to photocopy this figure is granted to purchasers of this book for personal use only. See copyright page for details.

this class then sang along with the recording of "I Had an Old Coat" as they used bingo markers and checkers to move to the key word of each new verse. As they did so, they lightly tapped the song's steady beat onto the sheet of paper. For instance, when the song text read, "I stained that *vest* with cherry pie, So I cut and sewed 'til I had me a *tie*," the children would rhythmically (keeping the steady beat) move their markers from the vest to the tie. As an added bonus, the charming sequence theme of the song "I Had an Old Coat" can be easily connected to the Caldecott Award-winning book *Joseph Had a Little Overcoat* by Simms Taback (1999), a Hawaiian version of the story found in *Auntie* by Stephany Indie (1998), as well as Patricia Polloco's (1998) popular book *The Keeping Quilt*.

In another classroom observation, a well-known children's song, "I Know an Old Lady Who Swallowed a Fly," was used to reinforce sequence. The lyrics began:

> I know an old lady who swallowed a fly;
> I don't know why she swallowed a fly. I guess she'll die.

The second verse continues with the lyric sequence "I know an old lady who swallowed a spider that wriggled and wriggled and tickled inside her," which then adds the first verse in a cumulative style. As they sang, the children held up small paper cut-out characters attached to popsicle sticks (fly, spider, bird, cat, dog, goat, cow, and horse) to show the song's evolving story sequence. On another day, the children sang the song again, this time demonstrating their understanding of sequence and their comprehension of the song lyrics by holding up word cards. Each card had an animal character name written on it, and the children delighted in holding up their word cards at the appropriate time during the singing of the song. As they did so, they were required to find the next animal in the song, read the names, and organize their cards in a sequenced order—all within the enjoyable contexts of active music making.

In other classrooms, two children's books that use the same sequence story theme, *There Was an Old Lady Who Swallowed a Fly* by Taback (1997) and Adams

(1999), were used first within dramatic/rhythmic group read-alouds and later as a visual prompt during group singing and creative movements of the song "I Know an Old Lady Who Swallowed a Fly." One teacher then added a CD recording of the King's Singers' humorous version of "I Know an Old Woman" within an extension listening lesson in which the children were asked to compare the recorded version to their song version. The children were delighted by the King's Singers' dazzling additions of the various animal character sounds!

Students can also learn about story sequence through a variety of musical listening activities. For instance, they can illustrate their ideas of a musical story sequence while listening to music. In Appendix C students first learn about the story sequence underlying the music they are about to hear. In this case, the composer, Smetana, composed *The Moldau* with a story sequence in mind and used a symphonic poem structure.

In this lesson, the teacher holds up large cards, reads aloud, and has the students echo each of the events on the story cards (e.g., "Deep in the forest . . . the little stream comes to life . . . "). The cards are arranged in left-to-right order reflecting the order of events the students will hear in the music. After the read-aloud, students are asked to imagine and illustrate events from the musical story sequence as they listen to a recording of *The Moldau*. Here, the student's sense of story sequence has been reinforced through reading, listening, imagining, visualization, and illustration.

PHONEMIC AWARENESS AND PHONICS

Phonemic awareness is believed to be a necessary precursor to reading (Adams, 1998) and an important component of a balanced early literacy program (Fisher, Lapp, & Flood, 1999; Yopp & Yopp, 1997). Accordingly, the Reading Language Arts Framework for California Schools states, "The most essential element of language arts instruction in kindergarten is the development of phonemic awareness; that is, teaching students the sound structure of language" (California Department of Education, 1999). Phonemic awareness occurs when students grasp the concept that letter sounds can be manipulated and recombined to create new words. Phonemic awareness differs from phonics in that the former focuses on sounds, not print. In addition to phonemic awareness, students must learn how letters are used to represent speech sounds (Lapp & Flood, 1997; Lapp, Flood, Moore, & Nichols, 2005). The goal of phonics instruction is to move children to automaticity—or automatic word recognition—so that they can focus on meaning rather than on decoding words.

Teachers of young children can use music to address phonemic awareness on a daily basis. For example, after his first graders finished chanting "Engine, Engine," a teacher pointed out that there were many rhyming words in the chant and asked "Where are the rhyming words? What are they?"

Engine, engine, number nine
Rolling down Chicago line.
See it sparkle, see it shine,
Engine, engine number nine.

Once children had located these words, the teacher listed them within an outline of a giant train engine. After all the rhyming words had been listed, the teacher and class created movements to each line of the chant. The teacher then led the class in several games to heighten their awareness of the rhyming words. One was to ask the children to look at the chart as they moved and silently mouthed the words of each line. When the children came to the ending rhyming word of each line (*nine, line, shine, nine*), they said that word out loud together.

What better way than music is there to provide young children a captivating entrance to the world of phonemes? Think of how we play with words within songs. Words are shortened, lengthened, repeated, sung high and low, loud and soft. Lyrics are rhymed and altered in many ways—all connected to language play or language development.

In addition to phonemic awareness, teachers of younger students must also develop students' understanding of the sound–symbol system, or phonics. One of the ways we do this is through the identification of basic spelling patterns.

Spelling remains a challenge for many students. It is important for early readers to understand that the English language has a number of word families and that these word families are based on specific spelling patterns. One of the ways that classroom teachers teach basic spelling patterns is through the use of word sort activities (e.g., Abouzeid, Invernizzi, Bear, & Ganske, 2000). Word sort activities include sorting words by first letter, by topic, and by ending spelling pattern.

With second-grade students, a teacher used the song "In the Barnyard" to teach and reinforce spelling patterns (see Figure 2.2). He had written all the words from the song that ended with -*alk*, -*ound*, or -*oud* on sentence strips. He asked his students to sort the cards by spelling pattern; all the words with -*ound*, for example, were to be placed in the same column. As a distracter, because he knew his students well, he added a few words that did not fit into one of the three spelling patterns and watched to see if students would leave those cards out.

FIGURE 2.2. Photo of sentence strips for "In the Barnyard."

Other examples of the use of basic spelling patterns in music are easy to find. For instance, in another classroom, a teacher used the song "Free at Last" to focus on the word sort for the spelling pattern -*alk* and -*air*. In addition to asking students to sort the words from the song, she invited them to identify additional words with the spelling pattern and write them on cards. When small groups of students had done so, they passed their cards to another group for this new group to sort.

Another useful and creative song for word sort activity, "I Can't Spell Hippopotamus," includes a variety of two-letter word families or phonemes. The lyrics to this song include many rhyming words such as: *hat/fat/cat/mat*, *hog/dog/log*, etc. Children are delighted to spell out loud and creatively move to their new rhyming word discoveries. One teacher we observed used this song at a listening station and invited her students to use the onset and rime cards to create lists of words from the song.

BACKGROUND KNOWLEDGE AND VOCABULARY

Background knowledge and vocabulary are necessary for later reading and writing experiences. As Rosenblatt (1995) notes, readers bring a great deal of history to the text as they read. This transaction between the reader and the text is highly dependent on what the reader already knows. Classroom teachers often use thematic and interdisciplinary instruction to tie their lessons together and build on background knowledge. Classroom teachers also favor vocabulary lessons that are integrated into their thematic lessons.

As Gilles, Andre, Dye, and Pfannenstiel (1998) point out, students acquire new vocabulary and are introduced to fresh content each time they sing a new song. For example, in the delightful story song "The Crocodile," some students may not be familiar with the song's words, phrases, and concepts (e.g., "Crocodile, tame as tame can be, down the Nile, bade them all goodbye"). During another observation, a teacher listed these concepts, discussed their meanings, and encouraged the children to think of appropriate movements depicting those meanings. As the teacher returned to this same song on another day, she created a large story map chart asking the children to provide the *who*—a lady, *where*—at the Nile River, *when*—on a lovely summer day (components of the beginning section of the song story), and *what* (happened)—the lady rode on the back of a friendly crocodile as she waved to people on the riverbank and the crocodile winked as he smiled . . . (components of the song text's middle section), as well as what happened at the end of the story. These kinds of early literacy/music teaching processes are a natural and frequently occurring instructional component prevalent in many classrooms that serve to heighten children's understanding of new vocabulary within meaningful, active, and expressive contexts.

Mrs. Laws was interested in having her students understand the concept of antonyms, apply what they learned to using a thesaurus, and "come up with their own antonyms." Mrs. Laws used an overhead transparency of the words to the Beatles song "Hello, Goodbye" with the antonyms circled. She invited her students to participate in a shared, choral reading of the song text as well as to follow along with the text as they listened to the recording. The students then worked with a partner to come up with movements for each set of antonyms and performed their ideas with the Beatles recording.

In another of her class sessions, Mrs. Laws had pairs of students rewrite the lines of the song (e.g., "You say big, I say little.") and add movements to their original lyrics. Mrs. Laws then brought in a karaoke version of the song to use with performances of the new antonym lyrics. Mrs. Laws comments on an incident that reflected her students' enjoyment and retention of the lesson about antonyms: "A month later, it was a very hot day, and a student said to me, 'I'm so cold . . . just kidding. I'm being an antonym!' " Another student wrote in her class journal, "I loved being a composer and writing my own antonym lyrics."

Our students' vocabulary can also be increased in a variety of interesting ways through musical activity linked with our literacy instruction. Mrs. Reilly-Feehley wanted to help her students "cement" more math vocabulary through creating a song using vocabulary about shapes (e.g., hexagon, trapezoid, square, cube, prism, sphere, etc.). Each student was given a bag of shapes. Using the familiar tune of

"The Wheels on the Bus," the class created new lyrics for each shape in their bag: "A hexagon has five sides, five sides, five sides. A hexagon can be made with two trapezoids . . . all day long." In this lesson, the students also created pictures using these shapes, shared their pictures, and wrote a paragraph about their picture. Mrs. Reilly-Feehly adds that her students thought "this was a cool way to learn geometry shapes" and that "it was fun to do art and math together!"

Let's look at a few more examples. In the integrated listening lesson about the River Moldau (see Appendix C), students learned new background and vocabulary about the progression of a river from source to sea as well as the geographical features of where the river flowed and adjectives describing how the river looks and sounds (e.g., "swirling, splashing over rocks and boulders . . . cascading over waterfalls"). They also applied their understanding of that background knowledge and vocabulary to their illustrations of the musical events as they listened to the music. In Appendix F, students demonstrated and applied their knowledge of new jazz vocabulary as they used a listening to jazz checklist and checked off what musical events they thought were hearing in a sample of recorded jazz. They then debriefed their checklist answers in a class discussion to compare their understanding of that new vocabulary (e.g., early blues, Chicago Stride, solo, solo with rhythm section, etc.).

FLUENCY

When readers engage with text, they must use a number of systems to make meaning of the print. We know that readers must be able to decode the words, understand the vocabulary, and have comprehension strategies for making meaning of texts. If they do all of these things but do them very slowly, they are still likely to have problems understanding and remembering the information. Readers must also read fast enough to get the sense of the sentence and paragraph. As such, we focus instruction on reading fluency, the number of words that students can read aloud and silently and how they add inflection, tone, and voice to their reading (Rasinski, 2003).

Teachers can easily incorporate musical activities to provide opportunities for increasing reading fluency. Mrs. Sandoval uses song lyrics within her ESL/ELL (English as a second language/English language learners) classes so that students will "be more engaged in the reading. They can practice literacy skills by reading the lyrics and their oral skills by listening to a song. Including music softens the friction often found within reluctant and ELL student readers." In her lessons, Mrs.

Sandoval chooses songs that fit or blend into the theme or mood of a book they are currently reading in class. For instance, her students were reading the book *Child Called "It"* by David Pelzer (1993). A song by Mariah Carey, "Hero," pairs very well with the Pelzer book. She typed the lyrics to the song on a sheet for students to follow. "During the lesson, I first read the song text. Then, I pass out lyrics and play a recording of the song. I guide students by asking them to listen and read the lyrics as they follow along with the music." One of her eighth-grade students observed, "I liked it when you put the music on because most teachers don't do that. Music for me is great because it helps me think about the story much better."

Mrs. Feistel provided creative opportunities for her students to create original rhythmic chants about various systems of the human body. Examples include:

> Nose, mouth, trachea at the top.
> Bronchial tubes, the air won't stop!
> Lungs, bronchials, alveoli sacs.
> Capillaries let the oxygen pass.
>
> Teeth, tongue, mouth are at the top.
> Esophagus, stomach, the food won't stop!
> Small and large intestines, rectum's last.
> Anus is where you let it all pass!

Within these chants, students could engage in multiple opportunities for fluency. First, Mrs. Feistel would say each line (clapping along with the beat), and the students would echo. Once the chant was learned, all students performed the chant chorally. The class performed the chants at the beginning of each science period for a week and then took a copy of the chant home and copied it as homework. Mrs. Feistel observed students' fluency as they were chanting and clapping repetitively. Because of repetitive opportunities, "the chant helped the students remember and retain the knowledge."

COMPREHENSION

When it comes down to it, what is reading for? We don't read to be able to decode or to see how fast we can process the words. We read to understand, learn, think, evaluate, and enjoy ideas. We call this process comprehension. While it sounds easy, teaching comprehension and modeling comprehension strategies is complex and extremely important. Students need regular instruction in comprehension, and they need teacher modeling so that they can adopt the strategies that good readers use, such as questioning, summarizing, visualizing, inferring, predicting, clarifying, and so on (Frey & Fisher, 2005; Harvey & Goudvis, 2000).

Mrs. Reilly-Feehley wanted her students to "learn about Christmas traditions in other parts of the world, and how these traditions are celebrated now in America." She wanted her students to "think about how the holidays are not just about receiving gifts, but also about giving gifts." The British Christmas tradition of Boxing Day, when small gifts are given to those in need, was the focus of her lesson.

Using the song "The Wren Song," Mrs. Reilly-Feehley read aloud the song text and discussed the meaning of the words. Then the class explored movements to help understand the text and remember the words. The class then learned the song and sang along with a CD recording. A discussion of ways to help those less fortunate followed as the teacher charted the students' ideas. Students then decorated gift boxes and shared them with others.

Music can provide meaningful avenues for deepened comprehension. In Ms. Oxenhandler's class, the understanding of a novel the class read was demonstrated in the following creative way.

The students were instructed to burn a personal CD with a minimum of five songs on it that they felt related to the novel in some way. Accompanying the CD, students had to identify in writing their reasons for each song they selected (i.e., Does the song capture a character's emotions at a certain point? Does the song symbolize the underlying theme of the book? Does the song summarize your overall reaction to the book?). The students then had to design a cover for their CD that was original, attractive, and related to the book. The cover needed to have an original title and list the songs and artists. Students were provided a grading rubric in advance. The students shared their CDs with the whole class and orally explained the connection of each song to the novel.

Ms. Oxenhandler comments, "I was thrilled with the motivation of my students to complete this assignment. They also got a lot of unforeseen practice in interpreting poetry in the process of selecting their CD content. I was delighted to see them really listening deeply to music and getting in touch with their own very personal reactions to it." These positive reactions were echoed in comments by her students:

"Can we do this again?"
"This was the best project I ever did!"
"Do you have any classical music we could use?"
"Whenever I hear this song now, it reminds me of the book we read."

WRITING

Writing activities cannot be separated from reading activities, as writing instruction is a necessary companion to reading instruction (Dahl & Farnan, 1998). To become literate, children need systematic instruction in both reading and writing. Early writing instruction should focus on mastering conventions like grammar, punctuation, and capitalization—not merely studying and memorizing them, but really conquering conventions to communicate a message effectively (Fearn & Farnan, 1998).

There are a number of ways that teachers can and do contribute to early writing instruction for students. For example, a teacher used the chant "Miss White Had Fright." After the children were able to clap and speak the chant together, the teacher asked them to write replacement lines for the third line of the chant. The following sentence frames were provided for the children to write a new text line for the chant; "Saw a _____ on a _____" or "Saw a _____ in a _____," or "Saw a _____ with a _____." The children then performed their new chants, adding their own ideas and creative movements. To extend this delightful writing activity, the teacher asked the children to write out and illustrate their new verses for a class book entitled *Miss White's Frightful Night*.

Another way that teachers encourage writing is to play music and invite students to illustrate what they hear. For example, a second-grade teacher recently played the song "En las Pulgas de San Jose" to her class. While they listened to the song, they sketched on large pieces of paper. When the song finished, the students immediately began writing about their illustrations. Clearly the music allowed these students to focus on their thoughts and reduced the procrastination time often associated with writing prompts.

Using song texts can also provide students with ideas for their daily journal writing. Aida Allen, a fifth-grade teacher, used "Where Is the Love?" by Justin Timberlake and the Black Eyed Peas to increase her students' vocabulary knowledge. As they learned the words to this song, she selected specific stanzas and invited her students to write reactions. Tino wrote, in response to the line in which the KKK is mentioned, "How can people get filled with hate? I don't get it. Does that skin color matter so much? Don't they get it? People are the same. They want the same things, a good life, friends, family, health, etc. It's true. Where is the love???"

CONCLUSION

Classroom teachers can readily address early literacy development through classroom musical activity. In order to help communicate this important information to other teachers, parents, and administrators, teachers may find it helpful to use the information listed in Figure 2.3—adding to it their own examples (song and chant material, texts, storybooks, poetry, etc.) of what they already do in their classrooms using each of the literacy concepts within musical contexts. Completing the table might help teachers begin a dialogue with others as they share its content with teaching colleagues and administrators.

The time has come to make known the natural links between classroom musical activity and important instructional goals in early literacy development. Within group musical activity, children learn as they read, write, comprehend, and express oral language within the highly active and engaging learning contexts music making provides. Let's connect what we already do (and must continue to do) toward furthering the development and education of the whole child.

STUDY QUESTIONS AND ACTIVITIES

1. Read through this chapter again and place Post-it notes near classroom examples that interest you. Mark ideas that make you think of musical activity you might like to incorporate into your own literacy instruction.

2. Are there other classroom teachers at your site who use music to increase literacy skills? At a staff or grade-level meeting, find out which classroom teachers at your school site use music in their classrooms and ask them to share those ideas and resources with you.

3. Where are the resources at your school site? Locate and review basal music texts with CDs and songbooks at your school site. Search for songs and listening selections linked to literacy skills, themes found in books your students are currently reading, or instructional themes found in social studies, science, or math units of study.

4. Make a list of three musical activities you would like to use during your literacy instruction. Discuss your ideas with an interested peer. Teach these activities and discuss the results with that peer. Did that musical activity increase students' participation and retention of literacy skills? Why or why not?

5. Find out if there are professional growth opportunities, courses, workshops, etc. involving music for the classroom teacher in your area. One organization that offers ideas for the use of music in the curriculum is your local chapter of Orff- Schulwerk Music and Movement for Children. Find out more about this organization by going to their website (www.aosa.org) to locate information about workshops near you.

Literacy component	Resources	Additional music sources used in your classroom (fill in your own ideas here)
Concepts of print	"Hawaiian Rainbows" "Ev'rybody Ought to Know" "This Old Man" "Time to Sing" "ABC Rock" "I Got a Letter This Morning"	
A sense of story and sequence	"I Had an Old Coat" "I Know an Old Lady Who Swallowed a Fly" "Oliver Twist" (chant) "Brush Your Teeth" "Hush Little Baby" "Farmer in the Dell" "Jack and Jill" (chant)	
Phonemic awareness and phonics	"Engine, Engine" (chant) "Ackabacka, Soda Cracker" (chant) "Bingo" "Apples and Bananas" "Button, You Must Wander"	
Background knowledge and vocabulary	"The Crocodile" "I Had an Old Coat" "Abiyoyo" "The Sun" "Hawaiian Rainbows"	
Basic spelling patterns	"In the Barnyard" "Free at Last" "I Can't Spell Hippopotamus"	
Early writing activities	"Miss White Had a Fright" (chant) "En las Pulgas de San Jose" "Abiyoyo"	

FIGURE 2.3. Literacy components and teacher resources. Idea for usage: Copy this figure and insert your own curriculum materials to share with classroom teachers, parents, other music teachers, administrators, and curriculum coordinators.

REFERENCES

Abouzeid, M. P., Invernizzi, M. A., Bear, D., & Ganske, K. (2000). Word sort: Approaching phonics through spelling. *The California Reader, 33*(4), 21–28.

Adams, M. J. (1998). *Phonemic awareness in young children.* Baltimore: Brookes.

Adams, P. (1999). *There was an old lady who swallowed a fly.* New York: Child's Play International.

California Department of Education (1999). *Reading and language arts framework for California schools.* Sacramento, CA: Author.

Clay, M. (1985). *The early detection of reading difficulties* (3rd ed.). Auckland, New Zealand: Heinemann.

Dahl, K. L., & Farnan, N. (1998). *Children's writing: Perspectives from research.* Newark, DE: International Reading Association.

Emberly, B. (1987). *Drummer Hoff.* New York: Simon & Schuster.

Fearn, L., & Farnan, N. (1998). *Writing effectively: Helping children master the conventions of writing.* Boston: Allyn & Bacon.

Fisher, D., Lapp, D., & Flood, J. (1999). How is phonics really taught? *Yearbook of the National Reading Conference, 48,* 134–145.

Frey, N., & Fisher, D. (2006). *Language arts workshop: Purposeful reading and writing instruction.* Upper Saddle River, NJ: Merrill Prentice Hall.

Gilles, C., Andre, M., Dye, C., & Pfannenstiel, V. (1998). Constant connections through literature: Using art, music, and drama. *Language Arts, 76,* 67–75.

Harvey, S., & Goudvis, A. (2000). *Strategies that work: Teaching comprehension to enhance understanding.* York, ME: Stenhouse.

Indie, S. (1998). *Auntie.* Aiea, HI: Island Heritage.

Lapp, D., & Flood, J. (1997). Where's the phonics? Making a case (again) for integrated code instruction. *The Reading Teacher, 50,* 696–700.

Lapp, D., Flood, J., Moore, K., & Nichols, M. (2005). *Teaching literacy in first grade.* New York: Guilford Press.

McDonald, N. (2004). Haiku: Active learning with and through the arts. *The California Reader, 38*(1), 18–23.

Pelzer, D. (1993). Child called "it." Omaha, NE: Omaha Press.

Polloco, P. (1998). *The keeping quilt.* New York: Aladdin.

Rasinski, T. V. (2003). *The fluent reader: Oral reading strategies for building word recognition, fluency, and comprehension.* New York: Scholastic.

Rosen, M. (1993). *Little rabbit foo foo.* New York: Aladdin.

Rosenblatt, L. M. (1995). *Literature as exploration.* New York: Modern Language Association.

Smith, J. (2000). Singing and songwriting support early literacy instruction. *The Reading Teacher, 53,* 646–649.

Taback, S. (1997). *There was an old lady who swallowed a fly.* New York: Viking.

Taback, S. (1999). *Joseph had a little overcoat.* New York: Viking.

Templeton, S. (1995). *Children's literacy: Contexts for meaningful learning.* Boston: Houghton Mifflin.

Van Laan, N. (1990). *Possum come a-knockin'.* New York: Knopf.

Westcott, N. (1987). *Peanut butter and jelly.* New York: Dutton.

Wood, A. (1984). *The napping house.* New York: Harcourt Brace.

Yaden, D., Jr., Smolkin, L., & Conlon, A. (1989). Preschoolers' questions about pictures, print convention, and story text during reading aloud at home. *Reading Research Quarterly, 24,* 188–214.

Yopp, H. K., & Yopp, R. H. (1997). *Oopples and boo-noo-noos: Songs and activities for phonemic awareness.* New York: Harcourt Brace.

Zelinsky, P. (1990). *The wheels on the bus.* New York: Dutton.

THE ROLE OF VISUAL ART IN LITERACY ACHIEVEMENT

In my classroom . . .

. . . I bring in the arts to show that learning can be fun and creative. We use both books and our imagination. When I had my students create their own diorama to display what they learned from a unit of study, I had some amazing responses. It made my year to hear this so early on: "I used to hate social studies, but doing it this way . . . I now love it!"

—Khahn Pham

. . . students are encouraged to express themselves and understand others in a variety of ways. This is only possible by encouraging them to use a variety of art forms. The written word cannot always carry all the meaning, ideas, and feelings a person is trying to communicate. Therefore, comprehension of deeper and higher thought and feelings are often only possible through another art form.

—John Goodwin

When my students learn through the arts, their hearts and minds open to new possibilities. They take greater risks and open themselves up to more. Kids will extend their ideas in a more meaningful way.

—Kate Anderson-Gray

CHAPTER 3 ANTICIPATION GUIDE

Before reading this chapter: A = agree D = disagree	Statements	After reading this chapter: A = agree D = disagree
	Visual art activities improve reading, writing, and oral language skills.	
	Visual representation of language is an expectation of instructional standards in English.	
	Art activities take resources I do not have in my classroom or school site.	
	I have the time and talent to incorporate visual art activity into my classroom literacy instruction.	

We classroom teachers are continually challenged to think of new ways to strengthen students' reading, writing, and oral language skills. Many studies report particularly strong links between visual learning and improvement in reading and creativity (Eisner, 1998). In his book *Arts with the Brain in Mind,* Jensen (2001) concludes, "of all the effects on cognition, visual arts seem to be strongest when used as a tool for academic learning" (p. 58). Other research points to the value of student's artistic response paired with reading and writing (Hubbard, 1996; Madura, 1995). To this Hancock (2000) adds, "Although written expression is difficult for emerging readers and writers, children can readily share personal connections through drawings. Visual representation as a language art has been reinforced by professional standards (National Council of Teachers of English, 1996) and should be encouraged and respected as a mode of response for children of any age" (p. 263).

Simply put, we know our students need a variety of ways to explore the deeper meaning of the words they hear, read, and are asked to write. Student art-making activities can provide those opportunities. "Just as a child's writing gives clues to thinking and learning, a student's artwork provides evidence of cognitive development. In fact, children who lack verbal fluency many be able to express ideas with paint or clay or may have their words released through art" (Cornett, 2003, p. 161). Not only can our students' words be released through art, but rich discussion and writing opportunities can stem from the viewing of others' artworks. But how do we classroom teachers begin to think of and implement simple ways to use visual art within our literacy instruction?

The intent of this chapter is to identify and define literacy instructional goals with specific examples of visual art activities that foster language and literacy development. We begin with a conversation about oral language development. We then move to a discussion of reading and writing development. We focus the discussion on concepts of print and the understanding of story structures, phonemic awareness and phonics, background knowledge and vocabulary, fluency, comprehension, and writing activities. For each of the following literacy concepts, examples of visual art activities are provided, shared by teachers whom we have been privileged to observe.

ORAL LANGUAGE DEVELOPMENT

As you recall, oral language—both speaking and listening—is considered the precursor to print literacy. Students need multiple opportunities to talk and listen in the classroom. Thankfully, there are many ways to engage students in oral language development, and students appreciate the opportunities to communicate with their peers about topics that matter (e.g., Opitz & Rasinski, 1998; Roskos, Tabors, & Lenhart, 2004).

Mrs. Ward's fifth-grade class participated in a unit where they learned about the culture of Native American tribes of different regions of the United States. The students formed teams and chose a region and tribe. They then researched the tribe and completed a graphic organizer on each aspect of the culture using the social studies textbook, trade books, and the Internet (see Figure 3.1 for a sample). It is important to note that the creation of a graphic organizer, by itself, is using the visual arts to expand thinking (Wood, Lapp, & Flood, 1992).

Following their creation of a graphic to organize what they had learned, the teams then created a sketch of the design for a display board about their tribe and region. They found historical pictures, created original sketches, typed informational captions, and created a title. Other class members then viewed their displays as the creators commented on their projects.

Oral language development paired with visual arts can produce very successful results in increasing both student involvement and language skills. Mrs. Ward comments that her students "used oral language while working in teams. Students also listened to each other and presented their display boards. This lesson was effective for student learning in collaboration, research, writing, and graphic display. I assessed student learning by the quality and accuracy of the displays and the contribution of each mem-

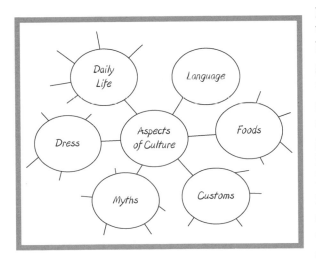

FIGURE 3.1. Graphic organizer.

ber." One student commented, "Are we going to get to show these display boards to another class?"

In another fifth-grade class, Ms. Allen used biography and artist study in her lesson about Pablo Picasso. Her intent was to "introduce cubism and abstract art and introduce students to a very famous artist of the 20th century." Another goal was to increase oral language skills by having the students do an oral presentation for a grade 2/3 class. Ms. Allen describes her highly engaging lesson in the following way:

"I did a shared reading using biography about Picasso from Kathleen Krull's (1995) *Lives of the Artists: Masterpieces, Messes (and What the Neighbors Thought).* My students highlighted important information. Afterwards, my students and I charted Pablo Picasso's important events. I showed students slides of Picasso's art, highlighting cubism. The students were asked to look in individual mirrors and create a self-portrait. Students colored their picture and outlined the illustration. They used an array of colors. Then they cut up their pictures and assembled the portrait any way they liked (to resemble cubism). My students then wrote a two-paragraph essay on Pablo Picasso and did an oral presentation to a grade 2/3 class."

In another integrated social studies lesson, Mrs. Ward wanted her fourth-grade students to "use their knowledge of the California Gold Rush to create artifacts that were authentic for what miners would have seen and used. Students could also choose to create visual art to show their understanding of the Gold Rush. Finally, my students could serve as docents and use oral language to describe their work to other classes." In describing her lesson content, Mrs. Ward commented:

"My students researched the Gold Rush using the social studies text, trade books, and the Internet. They chose whether to create a clay artifact or draw visual art to show their knowledge of the Gold Rush. My students then selected an idea and found nonfiction sources to help support their idea. They then created their clay artifacts or visual art. Once their work was complete, they displayed their work with a caption explaining their artifact. Their work was exhibited on display boards on desktops for other classes to come in and do a 'gallery walk.' My students served as eager docents who were very willing to explain their work!"

In evaluating this creative oral language/visual art/social studies lesson, Mrs. Ward concluded, "My students loved the opportunity to work with clay to create artifacts. My visual artists loved being able to show what they knew using art skills. One student exclaimed, "Mrs. Ward, look at our mining pans!" In addition, many other students at the school were inspired by the students' oral presentations and knowledge about the Gold Rush. History came alive!

CONCEPTS OF PRINT

As you will recall from the chapter on music, concepts of print include the knowledge that print, not pictures, contains the message, how to hold a book, the difference between upper- and lowercase letters, left-to-right print orientation, top-to-bottom directionality, and the use of punctuation marks. As part of a comprehensive literacy program, students can be taught about the way print works and how to use printed messages to convey their thoughts, ideas, wants, needs, and dreams (Pinnell & Fountas, 1996). As students get older, they understand the basic ways that print works but may still need to learn about speaking dialogue, effective pauses, and the like.

One very interesting example of how concepts of print can be reinforced through visual art activity comes from Ms. Tanonis's kindergarten classroom. Her lesson idea centered on some plain, oversized alphabet letter cutouts purchased from a local teacher supply store. In her lesson, Ms. Tanonis said she

> "hoped to take the traditional word wall and change it in a way that really motivated the children to use it. I wanted to have the children paint the large cutout letters so that they would have ownership of the alphabet and hang it from the ceiling. I thought that having the large letters hang from the ceiling would be amusing and interesting to my students and would catch their eyes every day. Then I hoped to hang words beginning with that letter on each of the large letter cutouts."

Ms. Tanonis developed her lesson over a few consecutive days, and the project quickly became a centerpiece for learning in her classroom. Her lesson evolved in the following way:

"I had the children paint the large letters. I tried to have the children paint the letter that was the first letter of their first name. We painted one side the first day and the other side the next day. Then I hung the large letters in alphabetical order from a string attached to the ceiling above their desks. I put them up in a snake-like pattern, not all in a straight row. Then the first words I hung from the letters were their names. Later we added many more words beginning with each of the letters and hung them from the bottom of the painted letters. The children use pointers and pretend phones made of PVC pipe to read and point to the alphabet. They sing their ABC's and read all the words under the letters. They associate our unusual ceiling word wall with the books we read."

Be forewarned! Once students become fully engaged in art activities associated with literacy, much excitement ensues. According to Ms. Tanonis:

"The kids *love* using the word wall! We had to go over the rules on how to behave with the pointers when reading the words. No whacking the letters or words, just pointing, singing, and reading. I assessed my students by observing them using the ceiling word wall during center time and writing in class. They look up from their writing to find the words above their heads. One student exclaimed, 'Oh, no! The letter O fell again!' (It got a little heavy from all the extra words attached.)"

For older students, many of whom have a well-developed or developing concept of print, teachers can use the visual arts to reinforce their knowledge and to stretch their thinking about print. For example, while teaching third grade, Aida Allen used woodblock letter stamps and paint to teach students about spacing between words. At one of their learning centers, students were provided with woodcut blocks, one letter per block. Using inkpads and construction paper, they were to write out their reactions to a painting that they had seen in a museum on a recent field trip. While the main goal of this activity was the reaction to the painting, Ms. Allen also wanted to assess her students' understanding of concepts of print. By using small wood blocks, she could slow their writing down enough to get them to pay attention to the spacing between words.

A SENSE OF STORY AND SEQUENCE

As we noted in the last chapter, developing a sense of story is important. For fiction, sequence also matters. As readers become more sophisticated, we introduce them to story grammar, the language we use to discuss stories and narrative texts.

Of course, you know all of these components—characters, plot, setting, action, etc. Graesser, Golding, and Long (1990) describe stories that have "story grammar" as typically including a main character who encounters a problem, sets a goal, experiences events while he or she attempts to achieve the goal, and either succeeds or fails at achieving the goal.

Using the book *Sweet Clara and the Freedom Quilt* by Deborah Hopkinson (1993), Mr. Pham created a literacy-through-art/social studies lesson exploring the themes of the Underground Railroad, slavery, and the African American tradition of quilting and storytelling through symbolic representation in art. Mr. Pham wanted his third-grade students to use landform symbols to create a map and a story. He explains his lesson progression in the following way:

"First, I read the story as a read-aloud. We discussed the outcome of the story and tried to decipher the map that was hidden in the quilt. I explained elements of pattern and design, such as a series of jagged lines or shapes to create the texture of the 'fabric.' The students were given 24 squares and instructed to make six groups of squares with four in each group (24 ÷ 6 = 4). Each group of four had to have the same color and pattern. The students arranged their finished squares into repetitive sequences and glued them onto 12″ × 18″ construction paper. Then, they used symbols to create their 'map.' Finally, the students glued 3″ strands of yarn at the cross-section of each square. (It's best to do this lesson over two days. On the first day, color, paint, and allow to dry. On the second day, assemble and glue.)"

During this lesson, Mr. Pham observed his students listening well to the read-aloud and participating in a lot of peer talk. He encouraged his students to research the African American freedom quilts and their symbolic "language" using the Internet. Through their direct participation in art making, students were able to share their maps and tell their stories through symbols. The class developed a rubric classification of the patterns and symbols found within each piece of art: designs indicating directions for the slaves to follow, symbols of key land forms, and distinctive patterns, sequences, and textures of each piece. Mr. Pham's students were highly involved in this lesson and very interested in the discussion of symbolic meanings within their peers' work. His students' understanding of story and sequence within *Sweet Clara and the Freedom Quilt* was markedly increased through their activity of artistic recreation of the story's events.

Back in kindergarten, Ms. Tanonis wanted her students to learn about geometric shapes, vocabulary, colors, and how to follow a list or sequence. According to the content standards, her students should understand the information text style or genre called "how to," which includes instructions and other ways to complete things. She integrated these two ideas (geometric shapes and "how to") into a unit of study about how to make a pizza. She also wanted her students to have fun in the process. Her charming story of this unit follows:

> "The students and I wrote a list with step-by-step instructions on 'how to make a pizza.' I helped the students write the list by stretching the sounds in each word as they wrote. The students shared the pen with one another and wrote number one = crust, number two = sauce, number three = cheese, number four = pepperoni, and so on. Then I cut out brown paper circles to symbolize the pizza crust, one size smaller orange circles to symbolize sauce, one size smaller yellow circles to symbolize cheese, small red circles for pepperoni, black ovals for olives, white squares for onions, green rectangles for bell peppers, pink triangles for sausage, and brown rhombuses for mushrooms!
>
> "Then I took a small group of students, and we assembled individual pizzas by following the list. I asked the students to describe the different ingredients on their pizzas. I made the activity into a free choice center. We sang many songs and read many books dealing with pizza [see Figure 3.2]. The activity was wonderful to get my students talking about pizza and what they would like to put on their pizza creation. They began to take orders for pizza from other students and their teachers!"

Gelman, R. G. (1999). *Pizza Pat.* New York: Random House Books for Young Readers.
Goodman, C. B. (2002). *Veggies on our pizza.* Raleigh, NC: Pentland Press.
Hill, M. (2002). *Let's make pizza.* New York: Children's Press.
Holub, J. (2001). *The pizza that we made.* New York: Puffin Books.
Maccarone, G. (1994). *Pizza party.* New York: Scholastic.
Pelham, D. (1996). *Sam's pizza.* New York: Dutton.
Pienkowski, J. (2002). *Pizza: A yummy pop-up.* Cambridge, MA: Candlewick Press.

FIGURE 3.2. Pizza books for the primary grades.

Ms. Tanonis assessed her students by asking them about their pizzas: "What shape is the crust?" "What color are the onions?" etc. She thought, "The activity was an excellent one for kindergartners. They learn best through play. It is hard to keep the center stocked sometimes because the students want to play with it all the time!" For Ms. Tanonis's students, pizza art became a real way to recreate a learned sequence or story of how to make a pizza as well as a way to learn shapes, colors, vocabulary, and art design. One student exclaimed, "Look what I made!" Another, "My pizza looks good enough to eat."

PHONEMIC AWARENESS AND PHONICS

As we have noted, phonemic awareness and phonics are an important part of literacy development. In fact, they are critical factors in learning to read. Younger students require instruction in breaking the code, while older students may need help with multisyllabic words. Importantly, phonics can be taught within the context of well-selected children's literature (Trachtenburg, 1990). We also know that phonemic awareness and phonics can be taught and reinforced using the visual arts.

There is a whole collection of alphabet books that teachers use to teach students the letters of the alphabet. Figure 3.3 contains a list of useful alphabet books. One of the things that teachers do with these books is ask students to see how the artist or illustrator used the letter in the picture. By analyzing the visual art, students focus their attention on the letter at hand.

Azarian, M. (2000). *A gardener's alphabet.* New York: Houghton Mifflin.
Azarian, M. (2005). *A farmer's alphabet.* Boston: Godine.
Campbell, L. (2004). *The turn-around, upside-down alphabet book.* New York: Simon & Schuster Children's Publishing.
Cline-Ransome, L. (2002). *Quilt alphabet.* New York: Holiday House.
Fleming, D. (2002). *Alphabet under construction.* New York: Holt.
James, H. F. (2004). *E is for enchantment: A New Mexico alphabet.* Chelsea, MI: Sleeping Bear Press.
Johnson, S. (1999). *Alphabet city.* New York: Puffin Books.
Metropolitan Museum of Art. (2002). *Museum ABC.* Boston: Little, Brown.
Micklethwait, L. (1996). *I spy: An alphabet in art.* New York: HarperTrophy.
Pelletier, D. (1996). *The graphic alphabet.* New York: Scholastic.
Rankin, L. (1996). *The handmade alphabet.* New York: Puffin Books.

FIGURE 3.3. Alphabet books.

There are several exceptional examples of these books. *Alphabet City* by Stephen Johnson (1999) is a clever book that uses city scenes to identify letters hidden in the things we would typically find, such as street lamps, park benches, and ladders. *The Butterfly Alphabet* by Kjell Sandved (1999) is a series of close-up pictures of butterfly wings in which all the letters of the alphabet can be found. And finally, Sleeping Bear Press has published a series of state alphabet books that provide readers with information about the state along the way (www.sleepingbearpress.com), such as *E is for Enchantment: A New Mexico Alphabet* by Helen Foster James (2004).

Mrs. Martinez knew that her students needed additional instruction on some of their letters before they finished their kindergarten year. As she was searching for ways to teach the letter *M* (one of the most commonly missed letters by her students), Mrs. Martinez found the read*write*think website (www.readwritethink. org) and a lesson on teaching the letter *M* developed by Melissa Weimer from Waterford, Michigan.

Just as the lesson plan indicated, she began her unit with a mystery box filled with things that start with the letter *M*. While the lesson called for the box to be filled with M&M's, Mrs. Martinez decided to fill her mystery box with different things that start with the letter *M*—monkey, mouse, money, mask, etc.

Consistent with the lesson plan, she read aloud *Five Little Monkeys Jumping on the Bed* (Christelow, 1989) and established a number of learning centers to encourage her students to focus on the letter *M*. She found, she had a reading center at which students could learn more about monkeys, a writing center at which students completed a comparison chart, a dramatization center at which students created monkey masks, and so on.

One of the centers was an art center. Students were encouraged to use the supplies to draw, paint, or sculpt different things that started with the letter M. Of course, at her teacher center during guided reading groups, Mrs. Martinez also provided systematic instruction and word study focused on the letters that her students had not yet mastered. She said, "I had to get them focused on the letters we still needed to learn. I couldn't just do that in one modality. I wanted them to do a lot with the letters that we were repeating to really learn them. And they did. Next time, I'm teaching all of the letters this way. They get it when they do lots of different things, including art, with the information."

Older students can also use visual arts to extend their knowledge of sound–symbol relationships. Nancy Johnson uses vocabutoons to teach her adolescent students difficult words that have multiple syllables. Mrs. Johnson starts by introducing the book *Vocabutoons: Vocabulary Cartoons* by Sam, Max, and Bryan Burchers to her students. Once they are familiar with the form, students create vocabutoons for the words they are assigned to learn each week. Using their visual arts skills, students analyze the word and what it means and think of ways to remember the word (see Figure 3.4). Incidentally, vocabutoons have been documented improving students' vocabulary knowledge.

FIGURE 3.4. Vocabutoon sample.

BACKGROUND KNOWLEDGE AND VOCABULARY

In his book *Building Background Knowledge for Academic Achievement: Research on What Works in Schools*, Robert Marzano (2004) argues that we build background and vocabulary knowledge, in part, on the number and quality of our academically oriented experiences. This is a profound statement. We also know that background knowledge and vocabulary are critical for reading comprehension and are directly linked with student achievement. As such, our work as teachers must ensure that students have multiple quality interactions with academic information.

Mrs. Ward believed her fifth-grade students needed support to remember the layers of the atmosphere. She wanted them to create a mural to show each layer as a way to link facts to memory. Mrs. Ward wanted students to use pictures and words in each layer of the mural to demonstrate the characteristics of that atmospheric layer. She felt that having the mural displayed in her classroom would be a great visual tool to jog their memories and vocabulary. Mrs. Ward describes her lesson in the following way:

> "We read nonfiction trade books or the science textbook about the layers of the atmosphere. My students took notes on the layers and their characteristics. They then worked in teams of four to six students to use supplies to design a mural representing the layers of the atmosphere. Students sketched their design on smaller paper first. They then created their mural of the atmosphere with clear labels."

Mrs. Ward comments, "The visual art contributed to my students' oral language, development, and vocabulary by discussing key vocabulary and how to select symbols to represent them [sic] on their mural. I thought the mural lesson was very helpful for my students' attainment of very difficult material. I assessed the students' learning by the accuracy of their mural." Her students were equally enthused by this project; one student asked, "Can we make another one of these next week?"

Mrs. Feistel was interested in developing ways for her students to show what they had learned about the original people of the five regions of the United States—their geography, their settlements, the structures they built, and how they obtained food, clothing, tools, and utensils. She wanted her students to create posters and display this information in both words and drawings. To accomplish this, Mrs. Feistel and her students took the following steps:

> "We used our social studies text to study the tribes of pre-Columbian settlements, including the cliff dwellers and the Pueblo people of the Desert

Southwest, the American Indians of the Pacific Northwest, the nomadic nations of the Great Plains, and the woodland peoples east of the Mississippi River. I assigned groups of three or four students. Each group chose four tribes to investigate. They created a poster grid to display each of those tribes' location, homes, food, and ceremonies."

Mrs. Feistel observed that the use of "visual art absolutely helped my students to understand the Native American nations. They interacted very well in their groups and were able to use new vocabulary and practice it daily while working cooperatively."

When we ask our students actively to create, display, present, and discuss visual art related to classroom curriculum content, we may learn many new things. Heightened awareness of what is lacking in our students' literacy skills is part of that learning curve for teachers. Mrs. Feistel continues her observation of this lesson with a balance of pros and cons:

"Overall, it went well. The successes were the final products. I hadn't realized just how artistically creative my students were. Also, they worked much harder on this project than on many other paper/pencil activities. They were excited to be able to learn and work in this fashion. The drawbacks, of course, were that in cooperative groups, some did more work than others. Also, the presentation aspect showed me that my students need much more guidance in oral language presentations."

In his fourth-grade classroom, Mr. Pham wanted to instill a real sense of geography and scale. He wanted his students to build a globe and explore concepts of scale and spherical graphing to locate real geographic places, such as California. By integrating the social studies curriculum and visual art, he had hoped his students would obtain a real sense of models and representations as well as mastering vocabulary associated with geography. Mr. Pham describes his lesson as follows:

"The students engaged the social studies curriculum by defining a place, such as California or the United States, in a geographical sense. By studying the overview chapter on model representations, such as globes, map projections, and conical maps, students explored key geographical terms. The papier-mâché activity of building a globe model verified the key geographic learning.

"The students constructed papier-mâché globe models by first building the sphere, then by painting on the key geographical features. They labeled the continents, the North and South Poles, the oceans, and major islands. They then proceeded to label the key areas of the fourth- or fifth-grade social studies curriculum. They finished by drawing the major lines of latitude and longitude."

Mr. Pham explains that he has taught this lesson on two different occasions and admits that the activity can take a lot of time and preparation. Still, he felt it was well worth the effort: "Both times the students were very actively engaged. They explored a vocabulary-rich content and worked collaboratively. Language was important in the ongoing assessment and the English language learners in my class did fine as there was plenty of hands on exploration." After the lesson, one of the students commented, "Now, I see why a globe might be better than a map."

Mrs. Feistel wanted her fifth-grade students to write an original poem about a weather phenomenon. She wanted her students to create their poems and write them within a watercolor background that artistically depicted that particular weather phenomenon. The catalyst for this activity was the poetic text within *Water Dance* by Thomas Locker (1997). According to Mrs. Feistel,

> "We read aloud the book *Water Dance* and discussed the illustrations and poetic text. I asked the students to pick a weather phenomenon and write an original short poem modeled after the short poetic interpretations in *Water Dance*. Once the poems were written, the students created a watercolor picture of their weather event. They then typed their poem on the computer and cut and pasted the poem on their watercolor compositions."

Mrs. Feistel observed the powerful connection between vocabulary development and visual art. She felt "this culminating project helped the students' literacy development by having them write with the style of the rich, poetic vocabulary found within the book text. They were also able to visualize weather phenomena from their own poems by translating them into watercolor paintings." Mrs. Feistel added, "The final projects were beautiful and unique to each student's personality and creativity. My English language learners get very excited about showing what they learned through the arts." One student commented, "I like to paint with watercolor." Another added, "We can use lots of adjectives in our poems!"

FLUENCY

As you may recall, fluency means reading faster, smoother, and more expressively. There are generally two categories of approaches to improving reading fluency. The *direct approach* involves modeling and practice with the teacher scaffolding what students can do and providing multiple repeated reading opportunities, often with a time pressure. The *indirect approach* involves encouraging children to read voluntarily in their free time and to practice reading with their peers. As you may have guessed, we believe that instructional time has to be devoted to both of these approaches.

In her middle school English classes, Ms. Oxenhandler works with students who come from a variety of language backgrounds, many of whom are newcomers to the United States. One of her main teaching goals is to have her students participate in English language conversations that give direction to their oral language practice. Ms. Oxenhandler "wanted students to start their experience in my class each day with an assignment that they can all be successful with, one that they enjoy and readily begin, and one that awakens their brains by requiring creativity and imagination. Additionally, the activity needs to be soundly educational and a springboard for conversations among students." She describes her activity in the following way:

> "As an example, before class I make a large drawing on the whiteboard (sometimes just the start of the drawing) and label five items in the picture. Above each drawing I indicate the assignment example, 'You have just discovered an animal never before seen by scientists. Draw and label it.' The students then pick up draft paper on their way into my classroom and sit down in their seats and immediately begin the assignment while I take attendance, etc. The students create their own drawings of the assignment and then turn to their partners. They converse about what they like about their drawings, what is similar, and what is different.
>
> "These drawing assignments can become linked to social studies and science content standards as well. For instance, a social studies prompt might be, 'Imagine you have traveled back in time to an ancient Egyptian city. Draw and label all you see.' A science example might be, 'You are a deep sea diver 2 miles below the ocean's surface. Draw and label all you see.' "

Ms. Oxenhandler observed that her students learned new vocabulary as they read labels on the whiteboard and within the context of their and their partner's drawings: "My students develop oral language skills and fluency through directed conversations with their partners." Finally, Ms. Oxenhandler notes,

> "All levels of students eagerly begin our assignment. By the time the last student is in their [sic] seat, everyone is absorbed in their work and quietly on task. As we do more of these activities, I see the creativity and imagination of students increase, and they become more comfortable with the associated

dialogue in complimenting each other's drawings and comparing and contrasting them."

Ms. Oxenhandler's creative ideas linking visual art activity to fluency opportunities not only immediately and successfully engage her students in conversations, but also result in revealing student comments such as, "This is my favorite part of my day."

Let's look at a few more examples of visual art activities linked to fluency skills. In Appendix E, students rotate through learning centers to develop expertise about terrain. Within one of the learning centers, students create a poster montage of a terrain and attach to it descriptive phrases and poems about that terrain. They also participate in a Readers' Theatre performance of a poem about terrain. In Appendix C, students use fluency skills in reading aloud and later illustrating the symphonic poem about the musical composition. In Appendix A, students use fluency skills in first viewing paintings about weather events. They then "tell a partner about a storm you saw." They draw a storm scene, then write and read sentences about this scene to their partner and to the entire class. In Appendix D, large group illustrations of each haiku serve as a background for an out-loud shared performance of their haiku poem paired with creative movement.

COMPREHENSION

The purpose of reading is to make meaning—to understand what the author is saying and to react to that information. The way readers do this, the way they comprehend, is by relating the ideas on the page to information they already hold. We have discussed the importance of background and vocabulary in reading comprehension, but reading requires more than that. It also requires skills and strategies. Let us illustrate this with an example shared by one of our colleagues. Try reading this list of numbers.

5942507	This string of numbers is hard to read and remember.
594-2507	This string is a bit easier because of the chunking of information.
123-4567	This is the easiest to read because of the chunking and your prior knowledge about how numbers work.

So, what does this have to do with visual arts? As we enter the classrooms of the teachers in this section, you will see how they use visual arts to provide chunking, structure, build background knowledge, and reinforce reading skills and strategies.

Ms. McGuigan wanted her middle school science students to be able to identify the various stages of the moon. In particular, she wanted them to understand the difference between waxing and waning moon phases. She created the following lesson by combining visual art activity with science study.

First she did a shared reading from the science text. In that text, students were able to look at a diagram that depicts the phases of the moon. Her students then took out a separate piece of paper and drew the Earth in the center. Then they drew sunlight by using arrows pointing at Earth from the right side of the paper.

The students then used a styrofoam ball on a pencil (moon), faced the overhead projector (sun), and lifted up the Styrofoam ball to blot out the sun (students were reminded that they were the Earth). They then turned in a circle and watched and observed the effects the "sun" (overhead projector) had on the "moon" (Styrofoam ball). They then recorded their observations on moon phases on paper with Earth and sun arrows. These students had to think in images of what the moon looks like during its various phases.

Ms. McGuigan adds, "The moon phases lab went well as the students were very focused on creating the phases of the moon. The students were assessed by reviewing their own diagrams that they created after performing the lab." Her students described their experiences by saying, "I liked moving the moon and seeing its phases while I turned," and "I learned that for a full moon, you need to go above your shadow when my back was at the sun." These student comments reflect their direct involvement in their learning.

Following the textbook reading and the lab, Ms. McGuigan shared *The Moon Book* by Gail Gibbons (1998) with her students. They were able to connect their prior learning—both the informational text and the lab—with the information this author was trying to share.

When Ms. McGuigan's students read informational text about moon phases, they may or may not have fully comprehended what that information actually meant. Adding tangible actions involving total physical involvement, experimentation and discovery, sketches, diagrams, and writing meant the students were able to think and comprehend what the moon looks like in various phases. The meaning of the information in their science text became immediate and real as well as memorable.

Ms. Tanonis hoped her students could learn about the famous woman for whom their school was named, Rosa Parks. She wanted her kindergarten students to recognize Rosa Parks's picture and talk about her with ease. She also wanted to combine social studies with visual art to make a large, torn paper mosaic portrait of Mrs. Parks; her students' participation in the project would "embed her image in their minds." Their lesson journey was as follows:

> "First we read many books about her life and accomplishments. We also watched a videotape with actual footage from that time period (1950s and '60s Civil Rights Movement). Then I drew a simple line drawing of Mrs. Parks's face on four pieces of tag board taped together. We analyzed the drawing and what colors we would need for her face, hat, and clothing.
>
> "We painted 40 separate pieces of paper with these colors. We added texture to our painted papers by using toothpicks, marbles, toothbrushes, and fingers with different colors of paint on top of the original color. When the paper was dry, we cut our paper into tiny pieces and collaged it onto the drawing with glue. We had to cut instead of tear because the paint would flake off. The whole project took about 10 days to complete." (*Note*: This 6′ × 4′ torn paper mural is proudly displayed at Rosa Parks Elementary School.)

Ms. Tanonis's students were understandably proud of this remarkable piece of art. Their comprehension of her life and times was extended by many literacy-related activities. Ms. Tanonis continues her story:

> "The children were good listeners during the video and stories about Rosa Parks's life. They were eager to know who this lady was and why she was so important that a school was named after her. We wrote in our journals about Rosa Parks and did interactive writing where the children write instead of the teacher. I only helped to stretch the words so that they could hear the sounds of the letters to write. We labeled our collage with our words when it was completed. Now, whenever they see her face, they say, 'That's Rosa Parks,' 'Rosa Parks is beautiful,' and 'Thank you, Rosa Parks!'
>
> "It turned out better than I could have imagined. I have never been so proud of a finished product by my students. Every one of my students knows who Rosa Parks is and can recognize her picture. I assessed the students by asking them, 'Who is this?' I would show them her picture, and

then I would ask them to tell me about her and her accomplishments. They all could do it and had a lot to say."

In a similar vein, Mr. Goodwin wanted his sixth-grade students to comprehend literal versus figurative meanings in the texts they were reading. He describes his lesson in the following way:

"I introduced the idea of figurative language. Using examples from current novels my students were reading and from their own slang, I wanted them to define and discuss the literal meaning versus the figurative meaning. The end product of this lesson was an 8½″ × 11″ piece of paper. The figurative language is written across the top. The students picked this language from a book or their own jargon. On one half of the page, the literal meaning is illustrated. On the other half of the page, the figurative meaning is illustrated. Each was labeled.

"The students presented their finished product to the class. Their illustrations served as a guide for their oral language and as a source of personal expression. The exercise of illustrating both possible meanings forces the students to analyze, interpret, and express the literal and figurative meaning of the written words. Actions of illustrating the meaning of the words and communicating those meanings to their peers requires critical thinking about a phrase in which the meaning and comprehension [are] otherwise presumed."

Mr. Goodwin's students were also asked to participate in a "gallery walk" and view each student project. They were asked "Did the student illustrate the literal and figurative meaning in a way that communicates well to the viewer?" and "Are the literal and figurative illustrations labeled as such?" Mr. Goodwin comments, "My students love this investigation into their own language. One student used the slang phrase, 'It's tight!' which another student chose to illustrate literally and figuratively!"

Mr. Pham wanted his third-grade students to comprehend that "water cuts through the land" over time. After reading about erosion, defining it, and observing a scientific experiment with cornstarch and water, the students were to recreate the effects of water on the land with a paper-cutting exercise. He describes their activity in the following way:

"First the students were given brown construction paper. Then the students drew a large mountain which spanned the length of the paper. Next, the students drew lines (rivers) and created large 'puzzle pieces' on the mountain (not to exceed 10 pieces). The students cut along the 'rivers' and glued each piece on blue or turquoise paper, in order, one piece at a time, yet not touching, to reveal the 'rivers' on the mountain. I told them, 'The quick workers may glue trees or clouds onto their projects.' The project is complete. My students wrote about the science experiment and art project in their social studies journals."

Mr. Pham was very pleased with the level of comprehension his students obtained. He adds:

"The students were engaged. It took more critical thinking than I had realized. They really had to concentrate to rebuild their mountains after they cut them. Each mountain was different, as in nature, and the 'rivers' were very visible. I assessed the students by the connections they made with previous lessons regarding erosion (either orally or written). One student simply expressed their [sic] joy by saying, 'It's like a puzzle. I like puzzles.' "

WRITING

As we have noted, writing is critical to the development of students' literacy skills and understanding of the world. Of course, we cannot simply tell students to write and hope that they will improve. Students both deserve and need instruction in writing across the grade levels. More specifically, writing needs to be modeled, and students need to be provided with scaffolding as they become skilled writers (Frey & Fisher, 2005). In addition, students need to write to learn. As one of your students will no doubt tell you at some point in your career, "I didn't know what I thought until I wrote it down." Writing clarifies our thinking—writing is thinking—and students need to do a lot of it to be successful!

Back in kindergarten, Ms. Tanonis wanted to teach her students primary and secondary colors using ice as a medium: "I also wanted to show the children that water can be a liquid or a solid and can be changed back and forth. I wanted to incorporate curriculums in a fun and innovative way." Ms. Tanonis explained her "Ice Art" lesson as follows:

"First the students and I read the story *Mouse Paint* by Ellen Walsh (1989). Then the children and I mixed red, blue, and yellow food coloring with water in three separate ice trays. One tray was full of yellow, one with blue, and one with red. We measured and marked the water line on each ice tray. Then we put them in the freezer until the next day. When we pulled out the ice trays the following day, we learned that water can become a solid (ice)

Mouse Paint

Ellen Stoll Walsh

and that it expands in this form. Then we took the ice back to the classroom, put on plastic gloves and drew with the three primary colors on white construction paper. Just like the mice in the story, we began to see the secondary colors emerge—orange, purple, and green—when they mixed with one another. When the 'Ice Art' was dry, we used a black pen and drew a scene on top of the watercolored page. Then we wrote a sentence together about their art piece. The artwork motivated the students to articulate what they saw and made them want to write. I worked with each student one-on-one and helped him or her to write a phonetic sentence about their artwork. They were eager to write and read back their sentences to me."

Ms. Tanonis learned a great deal about her students by doing this lesson. She added:

"The whole project went well, but differently than I expected. The ice really created a beautiful backdrop of watercolors, but I felt it needed illustration on top with the black line drawings. The students learned art and science at the same time and had fun while learning. While we were drawing with the ice, I asked the students, 'What is going on?' They all knew that the solid was becoming liquid again. I kept asking questions about art and science throughout the activities to assess student knowledge."

Mr. Pham wanted his fourth graders to explore the math concepts of congruency and symmetry as well as proportion, line, and form. He said, "By using a real-world example (art) of symmetry, I hoped to really bring this lesson idea home to the students." He describes this interesting lesson in the following way:

"First, I took digital portraits of each student. Next, I had the students draw a line of symmetry (vertically) through the portrait and cut. Then, the students glued half of the portrait onto drawing paper. Finally, the students completed the other half of the portrait by observing the contours and lines of their portraits in pencil. Once the drawing was complete, the students used colored pencil and watercolor to match the digital side of their portrait. The students then used the portrait to share their autobiographical essays. Also, the students helped to write the steps to the project in a shared writing (explanatory) chart before beginning the lesson."

Mr. Pham's students were given a specialized vocabulary to utilize actively throughout this lesson (e.g., symmetry, congruent, portrait). They also were given opportunities to assess the portraits within a class "critique" regarding elements of drawing: congruency, symmetry, line, contour, color. In this lesson, math and visual art content intersected, resulting in increased student vocabulary, comprehension, oral language, and writing skills. Mr. Pham added, "My students used observation and critical thinking skills. They used application of real concepts (e.g., symmetry and congruency) to create or recreate. They also observed the concept of symmetry in a 'real world' object (digital photograph)."

Ms. Oxenhandler wanted her middle school English language learners to "create their own original narrative story, one that they would be proud of and eager to read aloud to their peers." She describes her lesson experience by saying:

"Students were given magazines and blank storybooks assembled by putting three pieces of white printer paper together, folding them in half and stapling them along the spine. They were then instructed to cut out pictures from the magazines and then glue them into their books and create and write a storyline to go along with them. When completed, students read the 'books' out loud to the class in read-aloud fashion.

"The pictures the students discover magically spark their ability to conceive a story that they then read aloud to their peers. This generates oral language practice as well as listening skills as they are eager to hear their classmates' stories. In writing the words of their stories and reading them over several times and finally sharing them aloud, students gain excellent practice in writing and reading narratives."

Ms. Oxenhandler was surprised by the results of this activity and the writing that ensued. She added:

"I was stunned to find that every student could write a story when they were allowed to generate and string together ideas from pictures found in magazines. Prior to this, my students struggled to formulate ideas for storylines. I was also delighted with the variety of stories they wrote. Each one was original. It worked beautifully both as an independent project or one done with partners."

CONCLUSION

Visual arts are enjoyable, and our students know that. As humans, we make meaning and share thinking as we produce visual arts. The visual arts also help students develop their literacy skills in significant ways. Our students need to learn to read and read to learn, and they can do so with the help of the visual arts.

STUDY QUESTIONS AND ACTIVITIES

1. Read through this chapter again and place Post-it notes near classroom examples that interest you. Mark ideas that make you think of visual art activity you might like to incorporate into your own literacy instruction.

2. Are there other classroom teachers at your site who use visual arts to increase literacy skills? At a staff or grade-level meeting, find out which classroom teachers at your school site use art in their classrooms and ask them to share those ideas and resources with you.

3. Where are the resources at your school site? Locate and Inventory the following: books in your school library about art and artists, art-making supplies, teachers and parents/grandparents with active interest and/or ability in art, where to order supplies needed, etc.

4. Make a list of three visual activities you would like to use during your own literacy instruction. Discuss your ideas with an interested peer. Teach these activities and discuss the results with that peer. Did that art activity increase students' participation and retention of literacy skills? Why or why not?

5. Find out if there are professional growth opportunities, courses, workshops, etc. involving visual arts for the classroom teacher in your area. Visit your local art museums to find out about student art tours and educational outreach programs. One arts organization that places artists-in-residence in schools and classrooms throughout the country is Young Audiences. Go to their website (www.youngaudiences.org) to find contact information for your area.

REFERENCES

Burchers, S., Burchers, M., & Burchers, B. (1996). *Vocabutoons: Vocabulary cartoons.* Punta Gorda, FL: New Monic Books.

Christelow, E. (1989). *Five little monkeys jumping on the bed.* New York: Clarion.

Eisner, E. (1998). Does experience in the arts boost academic achievement? *Arts Education, 51*(1), 5–15.

Frey, N., & Fisher, D. (2005). *Language arts workshop: Purposeful reading and writing instruction.* Upper Saddle River, NJ: Merrill Prentice Hall.

Gibbons, G. (1998). *The moon book.* New York: Holiday House.

Graesser, A. C., Golding, J. M., & Long, D. L. (1990). Narrative representation and comprehension. In R. Barr, M. L. Kamil, T. Mosenthal, & R. D. Pearson (Eds.), *The handbook of reading research* (Vol. 2, pp. 171–205). New York: Longman.

Hancock, M. (2000). *A celebration of literature and response: Children, books, and teachers in K–8 classrooms.* Upper Saddle River, NJ: Prentice Hall.

Hopkinson, D. (1993). *Sweet Clara and the freedom quilt.* New York: Knopf.

Hubbard, R. (1996). Visual responses to literature: Imagination through images. *The New Advocate, 9,* 309–323.

James, J. F. (2004). *E is for enchantment: A New Mexico alphabet.* Chelsea, MI: Sleeping Bear Press.

Jensen, E. (2001). *Arts with the brain in mind.* Alexandria, VA: Association for Supervision and Curriculum Development.

Johnson, S. (1999). *Alphabet city.* New York: Puffin Books.

Krull, K. (1995). *Lives of the artists: Masterpieces, messes (and what the neighbors thought).* San Diego: Harcourt Children's Books.

Locker, T. (1997). *Water dance.* San Diego: Harcourt Brace.

Madura, S. (1995). The line and texture of aesthetic response: Primary children study authors and illustrators. *The Reading Teacher, 49,* 110–118.

Marzano, R. J. (2004). *Building background knowledge for academic achievement: Research on what works in schools.* Alexandria, VA: Association for Supervision and Curriculum Development.

National Council of Teachers of English and International Reading Association. (1996). *Standards for the English language arts* (p. 25). Urbana, IL, and Newark, DE: Author.

Opitz, M. F., & Rasinski, T. (1998). *Good-bye round robin: 25 effective oral reading strategies.* Portsmouth, NH: Heinemann.

Pinnell, G. S., & Fountas, I. (1996). *Guided reading: Good first teaching for all children.* Portsmouth, NH: Heinemann.

Roskos, K. A., Tabors, P. O., & Lenhart, L. A. (2004). *Oral language and early literacy in preschool: Talking, reading, and writing.* Newark, DE: International Reading Association.

Sandved, K, (1999). *The butterfly alphabet.* New York: Scholastic.

Trachtenburg, P. (1990). Using children's literature to enhance phonics instruction. *The Reading Teacher, 43,* 648–654.

Walsh, E. (1989). *Mouse paint.* New York: Harcourt Brace.

Wood, K., Lapp, D., & Flood, J. (1992). *Guiding readers through text: A review of study guides.* Newark, DE: International Reading Association.

THE ROLE OF DRAMA
IN LITERACY ACHIEVEMENT

In my classroom . . .

. . . I believe all my students have access to the literature in my classroom when I use art as media for teaching. Even reluctant readers and struggling readers excel when I allow them to use drama, movement, music, and visual expression to demonstrate their understanding of literature. Writing comes alive and stale writing becomes vibrant.

—Valerie Woodfillz

. . . I incorporate the arts into the everyday curriculum to increase oral language, comprehension, fluency, and to touch on all learning styles. If I present a lesson in more than one modality, I'm more apt to reach all of my students and the repetition of the same concept presented in different ways assures that my students will put concepts into long-term memory. Incorporating the arts ensures learning for life.

—Adrienne Marcell-Laws

CHAPTER 4 ANTICIPATION GUIDE

Before reading this chapter: A = agree D = disagree	Statements	After reading this chapter: A = agree D = disagree
	Drama activities take a lot of time to prepare and implement in my classroom.	
	Dramatic activities linked to literacy instruction take resources not available to me at my school site.	
	Student participation in drama activities can create more interest in oral language, reading, and writing.	
	My students are able to write and perform their own Readers' Theatre and plays.	
	Dramatization of stories results in heightened fluency and comprehension of the written text.	

At the heart of the art of theater (which many of us commonly refer to in our classrooms as "drama" or "creative dramatics") is its active use of language to stimulate our imaginations and deepen our understanding of the written and spoken word. We know that students come alive when given expressive opportunities to act out characters found in stories and legends, participate in Readers' Theatre, pantomime, participate in shared and choral readings, read aloud poetry, create dramatizations of what they are learning, and perform for others. Additionally, Cornett (2003) observes that classroom dramatic activity boosts creative thinking because "during drama, students must imagine, make hypotheses, test out solutions, evaluate ideas, and redefine problems" (p. 230).

Within dramatic activity, our students must also communicate, solve problems, negotiate, and cooperate with others by listening, speaking, and gesturing (nonverbal communication). Cornett adds that when students are engaged in dramatizations, they

develop fluency in language and nonverbal communication skills, use of the body, face, and voice to communicate. . . . Through drama, students learn how a look, a gesture, body posture, and how a person walks communicate hesitancy, excitement, or fear. We become skilled at what we practice thoughtfully. Drama is a pleasurable and powerful practice for self-expression through speaking and listening. (2003, p. 231)

We know that dramatic activity can also heighten concentration and comprehension in literacy. Students are motivated to read and write when they know those words may be dramatized in some way. Cornett contends that

when children are actively engaged and concentrating on a task, it is more likely they will understand the material being read. This is borne out in studies that show children who dramatize stories have higher reading comprehension scores than those who only read the story (DuPont, 1992; Henderson & Shanker, 1978). . . . Students who dislike reading see a purpose for reading that changes attitudes about putting forth effort. If students know they will be pantomiming significant actions of a main character after reading a basal story, they have a point of concentration: They are reading so they will be able to *do*. (2003, pp. 231–232)

Based on a review of available research, McMaster (1998) noted that drama is an effective medium for literacy development in at least nine areas. Each of these areas affects students' learning to read, write, speak, and listen. We will explore each of these research-based ideas about the relationship between drama and literacy and then consider the specific ways that drama can be used in the classroom. The nine areas identified by McMaster include:

1. *Students develop affect through drama.* Drama creates motivation for students to participate and engage in the learning at hand.

2. *Dramatization is a source of scaffolding for emergent readers.* When students are provided background experiences, they are more likely to learn content. Drama provides this scaffold.

3. *Dramatization helps students to develop symbolic representation.* Symbolic representation is the same concept required to understand the alphabetic principle.

4. *Dramatic activities provide students a meaningful environment for oral language.* In drama, students read repeatedly to develop fluency and have multiple opportunities to develop oral language skills.

5. *Vocabulary presented in the drama context provides students opportunities to acquire the meanings visually, aurally, and kinesthetically.* As students read and perform a piece of text, they use a number of different modalities to learn.

6. *Drama helps students acquire the knowledge of word order, phrasing, and punctuation that contributes to the meaning of a written sentence.* These fluency activities are directly related to students' comprehension of text and their motivation to read.

7. *Drama activities help students read different genres.* While many people think of drama as limited to fiction or plays, teachers know that children can perform and learn nonfiction through drama.

8. *Students monitor their own comprehension in drama and develop effective reading strategies.* When reading and rereading for a performance, students have to monitor their comprehension and discuss meanings with peers. They use their reading comprehension strategies in real time as they prepare for the performance.

9. *Teachers can use drama as an assessment tool.* Inviting students to produce a plan provides the teacher with immediate feedback about students' understanding of new reading materials.

Without further ado, let's get into theater!

ORAL LANGUAGE DEVELOPMENT

In addition to speaking and listening as we have discussed in the previous chapters of this book, students need opportunities to develop their own speeches and performances. In addition, they need practice in attending, listening to, and critiquing the oral performances of others. With drama, we can extend students' oral language skills as they produce their own works and transform texts into performances.

Mrs. Sandoval wanted her inner-city middle school English language learners to act out scenes from literature they were currently reading, write and perform skits based on text, and write and perform original skits that included an additional character—Super Chicano: Defender of Literary Characters!

Her literature selections included the following: *Holes* (Sachar, 1998), *There's a Boy in the Girls' Bathroom* (Sachar, 1988), *The Skin I'm In* (Flake, 1998), *The Outsiders* (Hinton, 1967), *Iggie's House* (Blume, 1970), *Party Girl* (Ewing, 1999), and *Esperanza Rising* (Ryan, 2000). This collection of adolescent literature explores the topics of racism, gangs, self-esteem, addictions, and adulthood. Supplemental reference books and science posters related to adolescence were included in the unit.

In order for students to write and perform skits taken from these various books, they needed to analyze and understand several literary elements, including characterization, setting, plot, theme, author's purpose, and point of view. By understanding these, students were able to develop skits. During the unit, students explored the various physical, emotional, and social changes dealing with adolescence as experienced by the characters and in their own lives.

Mrs. Sandoval describes the events of this lesson in the following way:

> "First, my students read the literature. As they read, they filled out a 'Book Journal,' which included a summary, vocabulary, quotes, and a personal reflection for each reading. My students would later refer to these notes to clarify the order of events as well as character development.

> "We then had class discussions and mini-lessons to analyze literary elements. I gave the students a Response to Literature Packet to scaffold literary elements (graphic organizers, etc.). Students were then placed in groups of five to eight peers. Armed with their Book Journal and Response to Literature Packet students selected a scene from one of the books to reenact. With my assistance, students wrote skits (to include a new character, 'Super Chicano'). For their final project, students were to present skits where Super Chicano, the superhero, meets the various literary characters and motivates them to overcome adver-

sity. The addition of this new character was not to alter the plot of the story. Students learned their lines and practiced."

Other classes were invited to see their performances. After so much engagement, students wrote responses to their choice of literature. They used their personal insights from their participation in oral language presentations. Mrs. Sandoval reflects that student learning and engagement in her literacy instruction were markedly increased. She adds:

> "By using drama, I contributed to the students' literacy development because they were fully engaged in reading, writing, and speaking in order to write and perform their skits for others. This motivation pushed them to carefully [sic] read and comprehend the literature, which later resulted in them being able to analyze the text at a deeper level. As they read, they wrote notes and took quotes from the text to validate their skits. In writing the skits, they applied writing skills. In developing their performances, the students had to discuss and practice their presentations, which added to their oral English language development. One of my students commented, 'Acting out the scenes was really cool because I got to feel how the characters felt. That helped me understand the book better.' Now my students keep asking when we will be doing plays again!"

Our students learn a great deal through using their oral language skills to discuss, negotiate, create, practice, and plan oral presentations. Students are motivated to use their knowledge about certain topics within dramatic contexts because they know their work will be viewed and applauded by their peers. During the process of preparing presentations, leaders will emerge. Group members will practice and repractice language in a very focused and meaningful way in order to contribute to the overall group effort.

In Appendix F, students participate in a dramatic literacy activity called "Getting to Know Jazz Musicians." In this activity, students work in small groups to prepare a presentation about the life and music of a famous jazz musician. They read books (biographies) about various musicians such as Louis Armstrong in *If I Only Had a Horn: Young Louis Armstrong* (Orgill, 1997), Duke Ellington in *Duke Ellington* (Venezia, 1995), Benny Goodman in *Once Upon a Time in Chicago: The Story of Benny Goodman* (Winter, 2000); Bessie Smith in *Turnip Blues* (Campbell, 1998), and Charlie Parker in *Charlie Parker Played Be Bop* (Raschka, 1992).

In this activity, the small groups of students are each assigned a jazz artist to study. In addition to reading biography, students research websites and other sources to create a four-part oral presentation. The first phase of the presentation is "We Learned about _____," where groups teach the rest of the class what they learned about their jazz artist. They speak, show pictures, add vocabulary words to the class word wall, etc. The second phase of their oral presentation is "Listen to Our Artist," where each group presents a favorite recording of their artist's music. They engage their peers in a discussion of the qualities of that music based on a checklist of musical descriptors (see Appendix F).

The third phase of this unit, "Our Artist in History," requires each group to create visual timeline of events and accomplishments in their jazz artist's life. The timeline includes student illustrations, musical descriptions, titles of pieces, and information about the artist and the era in which that artist lived. This timeline is presented to the whole class. Finally, the fourth part of this dramatic/oral language presentation is "Meet Our Artist," where one or more members of the group dramatize the character of the actual jazz musician. They may wear simple costumes and hold the actual instrument the musician played. Groups may create a simple paper mural background to create scenery for the musician character. The character then tells the story of his or her life and experiences making music. The whole class is then invited to ask the musician questions.

CONCEPTS OF PRINT

Concepts of print are not limited to understanding that there are spaces between words, that we read from left to right in English, and that sentences end with a period. As students get older, they learn that writers use print conventions such as question marks, exclamation marks, hyphens, and quotations to convey dialogue and different emotions.

While reading *Bridge to Terabithia* (Paterson, 1977), Ms. Allen noticed that her fifth-grade students were missing the conflict that the characters faced. Jess, one of the characters, faces several conflicts that come from within him, such as being friends with Leslie even though she beat him in a race or struggling with his fear of storms and water. She wanted to be sure that they identified the clues that the author used to convey this conflict, especially through the dialogue in the story.

Ms. Allen asked her students to reread specific parts of the book and to prepare for a performance of their selected parts. As she visited with each group, she retaught them the importance of understanding the difference between the dialogue (as the author marked it) and the regular text. She implored them to use their voices to "speak the punctuation" so that the audience would get a sense of the character's emotions.

Later in the year, during a unit of study on natural disasters, Ms. Allen invited her students to write short plays in which people responded to a specific natural disaster (e.g., tornado, hurricane, blizzard, flood, earthquake, forest fire). Figure 4.1 contains a list of books that the class was studying on this topic.

To ensure that their plays conveyed the emotion of the situation, Ms. Allen reminded her students about the use of dialogue and punctuation marks to "bring the people who lived the disaster to life."

One of the groups focused on floods. Part of their play read:

(*Phone rings.*)

WOMAN: Hello?

MAN: This is dam central. We're calling about a possible flood.

WOMAN: Is this a sales call? (*disgusted*) I h-a-t-e sales calls!

MAN: No, ma'am. We are worried about a dam break.

Aylesworth, T. G. (1980). *Storm alert: Understanding weather disasters*. New York: Messner.
Barnard, B. (2003). *Dangerous planet: Natural disasters that changed history*. New York: Crown Books for Young Readers.
Berger, M. (2000). *Do tornadoes really twist?* New York: Scholastic.
Duey, K. (2000). *Freaky facts about natural disasters*. New York: Aladdin.
Kehret, P. (2004). *Escaping the giant wave*. New York: Aladdin.
Rutland, J. (1980). *The violent earth*. New York: Warwick Press.
Sipiera, P. P. (1999). *Floods*. New York: Children's Press.
Sipiera, P. P. (1999). *Wildfires*. New York: Children's Press.
Thompson, L. (2003). *Forest fires*. New York: Scholastic.

FIGURE 4.1. Books about natural disasters.

WOMAN: Are you trying to sell me insurance?

MAN: No way, but we hope you have some. This dam is going to break and water might fill up your house.

WOMAN: NO WAY! (*said very fast*) Are you sure? What should I do? Where should I go?

MAN: Let's quickly review what you should do when there might be a flood.

WOMAN: YES, please, please tell me!!!

A SENSE OF STORY AND SEQUENCE

Understanding a story is more than getting the events and plot right. Of course, younger children need to be taught what to expect from a story or narrative text. As students get older, they begin to use their knowledge of story structures and grammar to make predictions about where the story is going and what might happen. However, their knowledge of the sense of story and sequence doesn't stop there.

As readers, we all react to literature in different ways. We all bring different experiences to the text as we read, and we all have different transactions with the text. As readers, we have both an efferent and aesthetic response to the text. An efferent response allows the reader to identify information from the text, whereas an aesthetic response activates the reader's feelings about the text (Rosenblatt, 1991).

Ms. Oxenhandler wanted to develop a way for her sixth-grade students to express the underlying meaning of a poem as well as their feelings and reactions to that poem. She wanted her students to know that "when it is hard to find the right words to express a poem's meaning, art forms such as dance, watercolor, and collage are valid ways of expressing one's feelings." Her lesson unfolded in the following way.

Students were instructed to select a poem from a collection Ms. Oxenhandler had gathered or to write their own poem (minimum of eight lines). Students were then asked to express their reaction to the poem or their interpretation of it in a quick watercolor, dance, collage, etc. They could also select music to play that they felt captured the spirit of the poem. This assignment was presented in class, and students were given one week to prepare outside of class time before presenting their poem and artform interpretation.

After reading their poem aloud, the students orally explained how their artform was related to or had emerged from their reading of their poem. In other words, the students had to transform the poems into a visual piece or performance.

Ms. Oxenhandler added:

> "This project works best when it comes at the end of a poetry unit so that the students have been exposed to a variety of poetry and are more comfortable with their own personal 'story' about it. One of my students commented, 'I used to think that poetry was so boring and stuffy—now I see that poetry is a part of everything!' "

Another example of dramatic participation in story and sequence is found in Appendix C. In this activity, students are introduced to the storyline (known as a symphonic poem) the composer Smetana chose for his musical composition *The Moldau*. In a left-to-right configuration, the teacher holds up large cards with text describing key events in the music (e.g., "Deep in the mountain forest, the little stream comes to life. . . . Bubbling, churning, splashing over rocks and boulders"). Teacher and students read these sequenced descriptions in an expressive and dramatic way before listening to the music. Then, during the listening and art activity, the teacher points to the cards to indicate where the listeners are in the storyline sequence of the symphonic poem.

PHONEMIC AWARENESS AND PHONICS

Understanding and identifying the sounds we use to produce language as well as the symbolic systems we have in place to record those sounds (printed letters and punctuation) are critical skills that students must learn in order to read (e.g., Adams, 1994). As students become increasingly sophisticated readers, their knowledge of phonics must extend to multisyllabic words (Blevins, 1998).

Mrs. Reilly-Feehley wanted her primary grade students to understand and explain common synonyms, antonyms, and homonyms. As she said, "I wanted them to gain a deeper knowledge of them other than rote recitation and worksheets—which they quickly forget. I wanted to develop an activity which expands vocabulary in a fun and active way."

Using the "Synonyms, Antonyms, Homonyms" song found on the Suzy Red website (suzyred.com/synonyms.html; from the CD *Chalkboard Songs* by Suzy Red, 1992) and the Magnetic Language Board: Synonyms, Homonyms, Antonyms and Vocabulary Building Pocket Chart Games by Lakeshore, Mrs. Reilly-Feehley describes the events of her lesson in the following way:

"We read the song on a chart and discussed synonyms, antonyms, hom-onyms. We then listened to the tune of the song (same tune as 'Goober Peas'). I echo sang the melody line by line (students repeated). Then we sang the song together. We then played a matching synonyms game on a pocket chart. I made a flipbook (three-section book) choosing three sets of synonyms from the chart. A child then chooses one synonym from the flipbook to act out in charades fashion for the entire class. The other stu-dents then have to guess the synonym they are acting out. Finally, students share the flipbooks with a partner. (This lesson can be repeated to teach ant-onyms and homonyms by using the same procedures, activities, and games.)"

Within this lesson, Mrs. Reilly-Feehley's students listened to the song text, read the song text, sang the song text, and acted out meanings of synonyms. She comments, "All children sang and followed the song text very well. They applied their knowledge of text both verbally and nonverbally by playing charades. Also, all students made flipbooks which demonstrated their knowledge of synonyms." Her students were enthused about this activity. One student exclaimed, "I like how we learned about synonyms—like that 'furious' means the same thing as 'angry.' "

In fifth grade, Ms. Allen noticed that many of her English language learners had difficulty with multisyllabic words. While she knew that she could not teach every word directly, she understood that she could give her students some practice with words and invite them to perform poems in which these words occurred. She thought that the addition of the performance would allow her students to internal-ize the rules of using multisyllabic words. Figure 4.2 contains a list of six common syllable spelling patterns that students need to know to understand longer words.

On one particular day, Ms. Allen invited her students to read the Lewis Carroll poem "Jabberwocky" (see Figure 4.3). She knew that this particular poem would provide her students with practice with multisyllabic words as well as with trans-lating concepts into their own thinking. Each group was invited to select a stanza of the poem to perform for the class. As Ms. Allen said, "They used all of their knowledge of drama to create the performance, but they really had to use what they had learned about decoding hard words to get the performance right!"

BACKGROUND KNOWLEDGE AND VOCABULARY

Far too many students start each school year without the background knowledge they need to be successful in the content standards they are expected to master. As a result, teachers must build background knowledge as they teach new content.

Once students have mastered the concept of the syllable, begin teaching the six most common syllable spelling patterns. These include:

1. Closed: These syllables end in a consonant. The vowel sound is generally short. (Examples: *rabbit, napkin*)
2. Open: These syllables end in a vowel. The vowel sound is generally long. (Examples: *tiger, pilot*)
3. R-controlled: When a vowel is followed by *r*, the letter affects the sound of the vowel. The vowel and the *r* appear in the same syllable. (Examples: *bird, turtle*)
4. Vowel team: Many vowel sounds are spelled with vowel digraphs such as *ai, ay, ea, ee, oa, ow, oo, oi, oy, ou, ie,* and *ei*. The vowel digraphs appear in the same syllable. (Examples: *boat, explain*)
5. Vowel–silent *e*: These generally represent long-vowel sounds. (Examples: *compete, decide*)
6. Consonant–*le*: Usually when *le* appears at the end of a word and is preceded by a consonant, the consonant plus *le* forms the final syllable. (Examples: *table, little*)

FIGURE 4.2. Six common syllable spelling patterns. From "Decoding Multisyllabic Words" by Wiley Blevins (teacher.scholastic.com/professional/teachstrat/decodingwords. htm). Copyright by Scholastic Inc. Reprinted by permission of Scholastic Inc.

The challenge is that students also need to understand the vocabulary necessary to discuss content. Thus, teachers really need to build background using the academic vocabulary students will need to be able to discuss the content. We know that all sounds somewhat confusing, but it is important. Let's see how teachers handle this challenge.

Mrs. Anderson-Gray wanted her third-grade students to be able to connect science content standards to folk tales. Her hope was that students would gain an understanding of the moon's phases and understand how different cultures might create stories based on their environment.

For background and vocabulary, she read aloud *The Moon Seems to Change* (Branley, 1987) and other nonfiction texts. The students then read the folk tale "Why the Moon is Free" from *Fiesta Femenina: Celebrating Women in Mexican Folktale* retold by Mary-Joan Gerson (2001). The class then discussed elements of the folk tale that reflect actual science compared to the cultural elements within the folk tale. The students created a storyboard of main events accurately illustrating phases of the moon throughout. They then used their storyboards to create and write a play that they could perform for other members of the school.

Much learning took place. Mrs. Anderson-Gray reflects on the student literacy skills used in this activity:

'Twas brillig, and the slithy toves
    Did gyre and gimble in the wabe:
All mimsy were the borogoves,
    And the mome raths outgrabe.
"Beware the Jabberwock, my son!
    The jaws that bite, the claws that catch!
Beware the Jubjub bird, and shun
    The frumious Bandersnatch!"
He took his vorpal sword in hand:
    Long time the manxome foe he sought—
So rested he by the Tumtum tree,
    And stood awhile in thought.
And, as in uffish thought he stood,
    The Jabberwock, with eyes of flame,
Came whiffling through the tulgey wood,
    And burbled as it came!
One, two! One, two! And through and through
    The vorpal blade went snicker-snack!
He left it dead, and with its head
    He went galumphing back.
"And, has thou slain the Jabberwock?
    Come to my arms, my beamish boy!
O frabjous day! Callooh! Callay!"
    He chortled in his joy.
'Twas brillig, and the slithy toves
    Did gyre and gimble in the wabe;
All mimsy were the borogoves,
    And the mome raths outgrabe.

FIGURE 4.3. "Jabberwocky" by Lewis Carroll. From *Through the Looking-Glass and What Alice Found There* (1872).

"My students' language was enhanced through their participation in writing and performing the play. Students read the folk tale. As a class we created a play (shared writing). My students had to reread the story (fluency) to create a storyboard. The creation of the storyboard helped them to think about key parts of the story and illustrate those ideas in connection to scientific knowledge."

By using dramatic activity to connect scientific background knowledge and vocabulary about phases of the moon to the meanings and storylines of a Mexican folk tale about the moon, Mrs. Anderson-Gray's students gained great imaginative insights. She adds:

"I've found that students have many questions about the natural world. This activity allows them to explore/imagine/create alternative understandings of the world around them. While learning science, they gain a deeper understanding of folk literature and how these stories might have come to be. Each student creates a storyboard and small group performance/adaptation of the folk tale."

One of Mrs. Anderson-Gray's students commented, "When I read this story, I imagined the sun wanting to marry the moon." Another added, "I think it's funny that the moon tricked the sun."

Another example of drama connected to background knowledge and vocabulary can be found in Appendix E. In this integrated unit about terrain, students first read books and sing songs about terrain (e.g., *This Land Is Your Land* [Guthrie,

1998] and *I Love the Mountains* [Archambault & Plummer, 1999]). The teacher then engages students in a discussion about types of terrain and the vocabulary found in these books (e.g., redwood forest, Gulf Stream waters, Rockies, lakes, plains, desert, Niagara Falls, Grand Canyon, etc.) A word list is created for student reference. Once the students have gained some initial background about terrain, 5″ × 7″ vocabulary cards can be used for homework. On each card, students list the word, the definition and an illustration of the word and write a sentence containing it.

Next, the students participate in a shared reading of the poem "American Panoramas." They add its new vocabulary to their word lists. They trace the route of the poem on a map of the United States. Later in this unit's lesson sequence, students write their own "pop-up facts" about terrain found in social studies books and other informational texts. As the teacher shows pictures or slides of American terrain, individual students read aloud their "pop-up fact" about that terrain (e.g., "Most mountains are formed when plates—giant pieces of the earth's crust—push and pull against each other. Some mountains are formed when rocks pull apart or break. Some mountains are formed by volcano eruptions.")

FLUENCY

Reading with enough speed to understand the words and with enough variation in voice to make the reading interesting is a hallmark of good readers. As we have noted before, reading fluency is the appropriate grouping of words into phrases that are produced with correct intonation, stress, and pausing. However, fluency is broader than that. It also requires students to understand and interpret text, make connections between the text and their background, and analyze critical aspects of the text.

Ms. Allen wanted her fifth-grade students to use drama to increase their fluency skills by reading narration and/or acting out what the narration said. She chose to dramatize a story from the Hopi/Apache cultures found within the book *The Flute Player: An Apache Folktale* (Lacapa, 1990). Ms. Allen hoped her students would exercise their fluency skills and "accomplish a greater understanding of Native American life during the Westward Expansion. I also wanted my students to make some personal connections between their own lives and those of the Hopi/ Apache Indians, especially since many of my students are first generation within the United States."

She paired *The Flute Player: An Apache Folktale* with "Daybreak Vision," Native American flute music by Carlos Nakai. As the recorded music played in the background, Ms. Allen read the book out loud. She comments on the progression of her lesson in the following way:

"I then gave the students the story on notecards. I chose four students to read the story aloud. I gave other students the re-occurring chorus part of the book text, 'Listen, it sounds like the wind blowing through the trees. . . .' My students then created a group movement for the chorus part. After a table read, 'actors' were chosen. Actors created movements and pantomimed action while the narrators read. My students created scenery and costumes. They were also asked to write about how the Hopi/ Apache life is similar to their own life now. Finally, my students performed this dramatized Readers' Theatre in a schoolwide history fair and shared their essays."

Ms. Allen thought that her students were "able to understand the life of the Indians much more than just reading our social studies text. Students were asked to utilize their fluency skills by reading, moving, and acting, as well as writing about the life of the Indians to show their comprehension of Westward Expansion." One of her students commented, "I will always remember the Hopi Indians after getting to be in the play."

A lower-grade example of dramatic contexts for using fluency skills can be found within Appendix B. Throughout this unit about transportation, students are building their reading and speaking fluency while engaged in singing (traditional songs "I've Been Working on the Railroad" and "Wabash Cannon Ball"), read-alouds and shared readings (e.g., *Train Song* [Siebert, 1981] and *Window Music* [Suen, 1998]), Readers' Theatre, lip-syncs of recorded music, narration, tall tales about imaginary trains, and out-loud sentence sharing about trains and transportation.

COMPREHENSION

The hallmark of reading, as you no doubt know by now, is comprehension. As texts become more difficult and information is presented in ways that challenge students' thinking and reading skills, teachers can use drama to help students understand.

Ms. Oxenhandler enthusiastically explains her ideas for her middle school class. She had a multitude of goals in mind, including the need to:

1. Deepen students' understanding of characters and their motivations in books they read.

2. Improve students' interviewing skills by formulating and answering thoughtful, interesting questions and answers.

3. Have students practice their oral language skills and demonstrate them before an audience.

4. Improve and heighten students' awareness of drama skills by incorporating appropriate costumes, mannerisms, gestures, speech, and facial expressions into their presentations of the characters they had become.

5. Have fun!

Ms. Oxenhandler explains her "Character Interviews" lesson as follows:

"My students were told that they were going to create their own talk-show and interview a character from a book they had read. Students were given time to select a partner and choose who would be the host, the name of their talk show, and which character (from a book they were both familiar with) the other partner would become. My students were then given five thought-provoking questions (e.g., 'Who was the greatest support to you?' 'If you could say something to another character in this story or book, what would it be?') that must be asked by the host and answered by the guest. They were also told to create five original questions.

"After planning and practicing, the students performed their talk shows live for their peers. Students wore costumes. I videotaped the performances and then my students watched and self-reflected on their performance."

Ms. Oxenhandler found that students were using comprehension skills by creating appropriate interview questions and coherent answers based on their knowledge of books they had read. She adds:

"I found the project extremely successful each time I've taught it. Students were motivated to do a thorough job of planning their interview questions and answers because they knew they would have an audience. The students loved dressing up and thoroughly enjoyed each other's presentations in which they surreptitiously learned about lots of other books. One of my students commented, 'I was really nervous about speaking in front of everyone, but I had fun and now I know I can do it!'"

In Appendix D, students select a haiku poem to recite expressively, create movements for, illustrate, and perform. During the process of preparing these short performances, students practice the haiku over and over again, discuss its meaning, translate that comprehension into movement and illustration, and fine-tune their performance to show the level of comprehension they have achieved. In addition to performing their own haiku, students get to view others' interpretations of haiku selections. Thus, learning about the meaning of haiku is extended through viewing and listening to the performances of their peers.

WRITING

Writing is thinking. Think about that for a minute. Can you do much of anything else while you are writing? One of the reasons we write is to clarify our thinking. Of course, we need help in learning to write, and we can all improve our writing skills. Regardless, when we write, we think and we learn. Let's look at the ways in which teachers can use writing and drama to encourage student thinking.

Mrs. Ward found that her fifth-grade students enjoyed working in small groups to write their own Readers' Theatre to perform for the whole class. She said, "In this lesson I hoped students would chose a person to research and create a Readers' Theatre biography to perform for the class. In making their own choices of people to research, students would have greater interest in the research, writing, and performance."

Mrs. Ward explains her sequence for this lesson:

"My students first choose groups of two to three and select a person to research. They research the biography of this person. Next they brainstorm some Readers' Theatre ideas and then write the Readers' Theatre. Finally, they practice and perform with teammates."

Mrs. Ward adds that in this lesson, "reading and writing together have purpose and meaning here." She continues:

"I loved my students' final Readers' Theatre performance. How great to know the kids had researched, written, and performed these plays themselves! I assessed the students in the quality of the writing and the accuracy of the biographical information incorporated. One of my students exclaimed, 'When will we get to perform our Readers' Theatre? We've already memorized all our lines.' "

Dramatic performances can indeed become a catalyst for heightened student interest in writing. If our students know their writing will be paid attention to, practiced out loud, and heard by others, they will go to special lengths to make their writing interesting to themselves and others.

In a unit for primary grades (Appendix A), students are asked to use their writing skills in the following ways: write and illustrate sentences about a storm they saw, write journal entries about weather events, and write a CNN-type narration for a performance about "Stormy Weather." The students incorporated their writing into a culminating shared performance featuring narration, singing, chanting, poetry, dancing, acting, sound effects, and action weather reports.

CONCLUSION

As you have seen, there are many ways in which readers can use drama to learn. We know that drama extends students' reading skills, regardless of whether they are performing, writing skits, doing improv, or listening to their peers perform. As the Utah State Office of Education (2005) aptly notes:

In a safe, nurturing environment, the arts enable students to express their feelings, communicate thoughts, explore their creativity, solve problems, communicate ideas, develop a sense of community, and appreciate themselves as participants in history, tradition, and culture.

What more could a teacher want?

STUDY QUESTIONS AND ACTIVITIES:

1. Read through this chapter again and place Post-it notes near classroom examples that interest you. Mark ideas that make you think of drama activity you might like to incorporate into your own literacy instruction.

2. Are there other classroom teachers at your site who use drama to increase literacy skills? At a staff or grade-level meeting, find out which classroom teachers at your school site use drama (plays, Readers' Theatre, creative dramatics, etc.) in their classrooms and ask them to share those ideas and resources with you.

3. Where are the resources at your school site and community? Locate and inventory the following: books in your school library about plays, Readers' Theatres, folk tales, puppetry, how to make costumes and sets, teachers and parents/grandparents with active interest and ability in drama, costumes at your school site and at students' homes, where to rent or borrow costumes and sets, where to order supplies, etc.

4. Make a list of three drama activities you would like to use during your own literacy instruction. Discuss your ideas with an interested peer. Teach these activities and discuss the results with that peer. Did that drama activity increase students' participation and retention of literacy skills? Why or why not?

5. Find out if there are professional growth opportunities, courses, workshops, etc. involving drama for the classroom teacher in your area. Visit your local theaters, university drama departments, and drama clubs to find out about student audience opportunities and educational outreach programs. One arts organization that places artists-in-residence in schools and classrooms throughout the country is Young Audiences. Go to their website (www.youngaudiences.org) to find contact information for your area.

REFERENCES

Adams, M. J. (1994). *Beginning to read: Thinking and learning about print.* Cambridge, MA: MIT Press.

Archambault, J., & Plummer, D. (1999). *I love the mountains.* Parsippany, NJ: Silver Press.

Blevins, W. (1998). *Phonics from A to Z.* New York: Scholastic.

Blume, J. (1970). *Iggie's house.* Englewood Cliffs, NJ: Bradbury Press.

Branley, F. (1987). *The moon seems to change.* New York: HarperCollins.

Campbell, H. (1998). *Turnip blues.* New York: Spinsters Ink.

Cornett, C. (2003). *Creating meaning through literature and the arts: An integration resource for classroom teachers* (2nd ed.). Upper Saddle River, NJ: Merrill Prentice Hall.

Dupont, S. (1992). The effectiveness of creative drama as an instructional strategy to enhance reading comprehension skill of fifth-grade remedial readers. *Reading Research and Instruction, 31*(3), 41–52.

Ewing, L. (1999). *Party girl*. New York: Laurel Leaf.

Flake, S. (1998). *The skin I'm in*. New York: Jump at the Sun/Hyperion Books for Children.

Gerson, M.-J. (2001). *Fiesta femenina: Celebrating women in Mexican folktale*. Cambridge, MA: Barefoot Books.

Guthrie, W. (1998). *This land is your land*. New York: Little, Brown.

Henderson, L., & Shanker, L. (1978). The use of interpretive dramatics versus basal reader workbooks. *Reading World, 17*, 239–243.

Hinton, S. E. (1967). *The outsiders*. New York: Viking Press.

Lacapa, M. (1990). *The flute player: An Apache folktale*. Flagstaff, AZ: Northland.

McMaster, J. C. (1998). "Doing" literature: Using drama to build literacy. *The Reading Teacher, 51*, 574–584.

Orgill, R. (1997). *If I only had a horn*. New York: Houghton Mifflin.

Paterson, K. (1977). *Bridge to Terabithia*. New York: Crowell.

Raschka, C. (1992). *Charlie Parker played be bop*. New York: Orchard.

Rosenblatt, L. M. (1991). Literature—S.O.S.! *Language Arts, 68*, 444–448.

Ryan, P. M. (2000). *Esperanza rising*. New York: Scholastic.

Sachar, L. (1988). *There's a boy in the girls' bathroom*. New York: Yearling.

Sachar, L. (1998). *Holes*. New York: Farrar, Straus and Giroux.

Siebert, D. (1981). *Train song*. New York: HarperCollins.

Suen, A. (1998). *Window music*. New York: Viking.

Utah State Office of Education. (2005, February 23). *Elementary fine arts core curriculum resources*. Available at www.usoe.k12.ut.us/curr/FineArt/Core_Curriculum/Elementary/default.htm

Venezia, M. (1995). *Duke Ellington*. New York: Children's Press.

Winter, J. (2000). *Once upon a time in Chicago: The story of Benny Goodman*. New York: Hyperion.

CHAPTER 5

THE ROLE OF DANCE AND MOVEMENT IN LITERACY ACHIEVEMENT

In my classroom . . .

. . . students have the opportunity to choose from a variety of the arts to express their thinking and comprehension of literature. Students smile on a regular basis because we dance, sing, act, draw, and create. Students tell they love performing.

—Andy Soto

. . . I engage my students by using the arts. Students are able to internalize and connect with the content when they are able to create their own movement interpretation.

—Aida Allen

CHAPTER 5 ANTICIPATION GUIDE

Before reading this chapter: A = agree D = disagree	Statements	After reading this chapter: A = agree D = disagree
	Students learn best while seated in their own seats.	
	I feel comfortable with the idea of leading my students in creative movement and dance.	
	I have students who may be kinesthetic learners.	
	Kinesthetic experiences increase student learning.	
	Movement and dance experiences should be geared toward performance.	
	I know a variety of ways to link movement to learning within my classroom curriculum.	

Have you ever watched what happens when children enjoy free time on the playground or in our classrooms? They investigate their world with motion, imagination, experimentation, and play. Their natural mode of learning and interacting with their world is not in a seated, stationary position, yet that is what happens in most classrooms. Jensen (2001) adds that

though we can learn while sitting, it turns out that the typical notion of sitting in chairs for an extended time may be misguided. The human body, for the last thousand generations, has primarily been walking, sleeping, leaning, running, doing, or squatting. (p. 95)

Similarly, Howard Gardner (1999) said,

I believe in action and activity. The brain learns best and retains most when the organism is actively involved in exploring physical sites and materials and asking questions to which it actually craves answers. Merely passive experiences tend to attenuate and have little lasting impact. (p. 82)

Jensen (2001) also points to the fact that sitting creates fatigue, restlessness, and sometimes the inability to concentrate or focus, which can, and usually does, result in discipline problems and class disruptions. None of us would argue with that. However, if the answer is to get our students out of their chairs and active during literacy instruction, we might first need to take a look at the value of what can be learned through movement.

Dance (which is organized and aesthetic movement) and creative movement are kinesthetic arts, which, according to Jensen,

play a powerful role as universal language, with a symbolic way of representing the world. They let us communicate with others, demonstrate human experiences, show insights, and solve common problems. Kinesthetic arts also allow us to better understand other cultures and provide for our health and emotional expression. (2001, p. 71)

Stated another way, movement helps humanize and broaden our communication efforts. When we move, we must work with others and show what we know in ways that go beyond and/or augment spoken language. Another important fact is that when students are engaged in movement and dance, they are using most of their brain. According to Jensen, when human beings move, we must

make rapid decisions, keep our attention up, monitor our emotions, remember our past, be alert of potential problems, create solutions on the spot, keep our balance, watch the expression of other faces, move quickly and gracefully—and somehow still remember the point of the activity. All these locomotor, manipulative, and cognitive activities are linked with developmental stages and academic learning at each grade level (Corso, 1997). (2001, p. 72)

Jensen divides types of learning into two very broad areas. The first, *explicit* learning, is the most common mode in many classrooms. Explicit learning is used when we read, write, and talk and learn from textbooks, videos, lectures, pictures, and discussion. Another whole mode of learning is *implicit* learning, which includes

a more hands-on approach, more trial-and-error, habits, role plays, life experience, drama, experiential learning, games, and active learning. Researchers believe that implicit learning is, in fact, much more reliable than the old-style classroom education that emphasizes reading textbooks and memorizing facts. (Reber, 1993, as quoted in Jensen, 2001, p. 74)

Okay, Okay! So we know children need to move to learn, but many of us may feel very self-conscious about modeling movement and dance for our students within our literacy instruction. How much extra time is this going to take? Most of us have not seen models of how to incorporate movement into classroom instruction. Adding to that mix, we might not know how to get our students up and moving without chaos ensuing! Cornett (2003) points out that it is a waste of time for educators to fret unrealistically about these concerns:

It is more useful to acknowledge ways movement is important in daily life and move on to finding strategies to put kinesthetic ways of knowing into action in creative and artistic ways. Most important is to start with a foundational truth—*we all love to move*. It feels good to walk, run, stretch, wiggle, and shake. It is also worthwhile to remember that what we *do* is remembered more easily that what is told to us or what we read about. (p. 289)

It is in the spirit of that simple fact—"we all love to move"—that we begin our discussion of how real teachers have effectively used movement as a powerful way of teaching, learning, and knowing within their classroom literacy instruction. Let's move on!

ORAL LANGUAGE DEVELOPMENT

As you recall, oral language focuses on speaking and listening skills. We know that these skills are critical to students' overall literacy development as well as important in their understanding of the ways humans communicate. Through practice, we all improve our speaking and listening skills; these skills are not fully developed when we leave early childhood.

Mr. Javier wanted his fifth-grade students to understand the ideas and goals of the 1950s and '60s Civil Rights movement led by the Reverend Dr. Martin Luther

King, Jr. After reading aloud the book *Martin's Big Words* (Rappaport, 2001), he chose a chant from a music basal text series for his students to learn (Silver Burdett's "Music Connection," ©1995, grade 4, CD 8-11). The words of that chant are:

> *Refrain:* "Martin Luther King, Martin Luther King, Martin Luther K . . . I . . . N . . . G, Martin Luther King." (Repeat whole phrase again.)
> *Verse:* "Justice, Equal Rights, Liberty, and Freedom . . . He had a dream that we shall overcome." (Repeat verse again, then go back to the refrain.)

Mr. Javier listened to the CD recording of the rap-style chant several times and decided to add some simple rhythmic body-percussion movement to help his students remember the words and rhythms and add expression and meaning to the chant. He added four thigh slaps on "Mar-tin Luth-er" and a clap on "King" and also claps on each of the letters, "K . . . I . . . N . . . G." (Try it yourself, right now!) Mr. Javier led his students slowly, and once they had mastered the words and body-percussion pattern on the refrain, he led them at a faster tempo. Then he asked the students to begin the refrain softly and make their movement and volume get louder and bigger during each recitation of Dr. King's name.

Mr. Javier also knew he wanted his students to focus on the "big ideas" of the Civil Rights Movement, "Justice, Equal Rights, Liberty, and Freedom." First he had the students chant the verse with these words. He then asked each of his students

to write those important words on four large cards. On the back of each card, students wrote what that word meant to them. The students then held up their word card and read aloud to the class what they had written on the back. One of the students wrote, "Justice means that the truth should win over the lies. It means you get what you deserve and it means things should be fair." Another wrote, "Equal Rights means you have to learn to respect people and ideas you might not agree with because people have the right to be treated equally no matter what color they are, what language they speak, or what they believe." Yet another student wrote, "Freedom is waking up in the morning and knowing you are safe and can live your life in a good way."

After a discussion of the students' ideas, Mr. Javier used the CD recording to help the students perform the entire chant. During the verse ("Justice, Equal Rights, Liberty, and Freedom"), each student held up the appropriate word card as they chanted each word. Finally the students performed their chant and read aloud their word cards in an informal performance for another fifth-grade class.

Mr. Javier commented:

> "My students need history to come alive. Dr. Martin Luther King will now always be remembered because the students chanted his name over and over again, learned important concepts of the Civil Rights Movement, and had a chance to write and speak about those concepts in a personal and powerful way. Historical figures can seem very removed from a young person's reality. This chant and movement and our writing and speaking made everything come alive for the students. By the way, the kids like this chant so much, most of the school now knows it!"

In Appendix A, primary students are taught a highly rhythmic poem entitled "Windshield Wipers" by Mary Ann Hoberman (found in Silver Burdett's "Making Music," © 2005, grade 1, p. 11, CD 1-13; see Figure 5.1).

The teacher first read the words from a wall chart and then had the students do the same. As they listened to the CD recording of this poem, they noted the differences between the first and second time the poem was chanted. The second time, the tempo was faster. (One of the students said, "That's because the driver turned the wipers on to high!") The teacher realized the students needed to move as they chanted. They developed a simple windshield wiper beat (both arms extended with bent elbows, forearms swishing to the left and then right, or meeting in the center) as they chanted the poem with this steady beat. The teacher provided a steady beat on a woodblock. The second time through, the beat became faster and the students were challenged to say the words and move to the "high-speed" windshield wipers.

Movement can be powerfully and memorably paired with oral language. Our students love to move. Their active involvement in movement causes them to be more interested in learning words

> Windshield wipers wipe the windshield
> Wipe the water off the pane
>
> | This way | That way |
> | This way | That way |
> | This way | That way |
>
> In the rain.

FIGURE 5.1. "Windshield Wipers" poem.

and in using expressive speech and voice inflection and aids their enjoyment, comprehension, and memory of the text.

CONCEPTS OF PRINT

Understanding that all languages use certain specific conventions helps readers develop the automaticity they need to be effective, proficient readers. While there are many different processes required to develop rapid ability to read print, including decoding and fluency, understanding how print works is critical.

How can we use movement to reinforce concepts of print? Students can become better observers of subtle differences in print through participation in movement games. One effective game is to have students slowly mirror the teacher's movement, noticing every subtle change and variation.

Ms. Frey wanted her very active primary students to calm down, focus, and learn to pay attention. They needed to be ready for their reading lesson. Ms. Frey found her students needed some kind of game or activity to get them out of their seats, yet remain quiet and focused to prepare for literacy instruction.

Ms. Frey began her movement lesson by playing a recording of very quiet, soothing music. She chose Japanese flute (*shakuhachi*) music to use as a background for very slow and connected movements. Students were invited to stand up and face their teacher. They then began to mirror exactly her moves, which were still very slow and connected (slow-motion movements). After they had mastered mirroring their teacher, students were then asked to pick and face a partner (without talking). One of the partners then began to move in a very slow and controlled manner, with their partner mirroring them. Then they switched roles. Students moved across the room with their partner in slow motion. Every student had a chance to lead and to follow.

During the lesson, Ms. Frey noticed the following:

> "My students became very adept in every subtle change of direction and motion. They were completely focused on either leading or following and did so in a beautiful and graceful manner. The room was completely silent except for the sound of soothing music. My students were calmed down, quiet, and ready to focus on their reading. All it took was a simple 5-minute movement break. One of my students commented, 'I feel better than I did before.' Another said, 'I had to really pay attention to what direction my partner was going.'"

By leading and following directional changes, students were using the same kind of visual discrimination needed when reading. The important additional bonus of this activity was that students were energized and quietly focused on the total body involvement needed to mirror their partners' movements. Ms. Frey concluded, "My students were ready to read, because they were focused and had a movement break. I need more of these activities for my classroom."

Ms. Allen wanted her fifth-grade students to respond nonverbally to visual cues. She wanted them to have a movement break that was fun, structured, and focused. She used a game called "Stickpeople" and describes the activity in the following way (see Figure 5.2 for sample cards):

> "First, I designed about 15 different poses or positions for a stickman figure. I drew each stickman pose on large colored paper with a dark magic marker. Sometimes the stickman was standing, sometimes, bent, etc. I tried to include some very subtle changes like bent elbows, one-legged poses, frowning face or smiling face, straight or bent knees, etc. Each card had a particular personality to it! I arranged the cards in degree of complexity, easy poses to harder poses. Then I created a game. I use this game whenever we need a movement break. When my students hear me ring the bell (like they have at hotel registration desks) they simply push their chairs in and stand up behind their chairs and face me. No talking!
>
> "I hold up a stickman card and they cannot move to that shape until they hear the next bell. So, they have to study the card and pick up on all the directions and cues within the figure. I ring the bell and they must move to that shape. Then a new card, study, and finally another bell. Sometimes I make them hold a stickman card shape for a long time, sometimes I change very quickly. It all makes for a lot of fun, focus, and a break from their seat work. They were energized and ready to read after our movement break."

Ms. Allen hadn't realized how much her students would enjoy moving. She continues:

> "I've never thought of myself as a dancer or movement teacher, as I've always been self-conscious about dancing. I also thought my fifth-graders would think movement was boring. But this was easy and fun to do. The kids love the game so much, they became choreographers! They designed their own cards and like to create dances where they hold each stickman pose for eight steady beats and move to the next pose for eight steady beats, etc. One day we covered the classroom walls with all their stickman poses and moved to each pose (eight beats each) by using a CD recording of coun-

FIGURE 5.2. Stickpeople cards.

From *Teaching Literacy through the Arts* by Nan L. McDonald and Douglas Fisher. Copyright 2006 by The Guilford Press. Permission to photocopy this figure is granted to purchasers of this book for personal use only. See copyright page for details.

try western linedance music in the background to establish a steady beat! It was great. Who knew my students would be so into dance?"

A SENSE OF STORY AND SEQUENCE

In addition to understanding the ways in which print works, students need to develop a sense of the story and come to expect that characters will develop, plots will thicken, and conflicts will be addressed. As students learn about a sense of story, they have to develop an understanding that things often happen in a specific order—an order that focuses on time or chronology.

Dr. McDonald wanted to develop a created dance activity that could then extend into visual art and writing activities. She wanted her middle school students to develop their own ideas for a dance. She decided to base her activity on colors because middle school students could easily relate to differences in colors and their effect. She describes her "color dance" activity in the following way:

"First, I asked my students to close their eyes and listen. I told a story about how I always remember colors. I described a rich purple color I once saw at the end of a spectacular sunset over the Pacific Ocean. It was a warm summer evening. I sat in a beach chair and watched as the colors of that sunset ranged from hot orange to red, to pinks, mauves, and purples. That purple was etched in my memory forever. I asked them to open their eyes and find a place in the room where they had space to move without bumping into furniture or other students. I established expectations for behavior and asked them to close their eyes and follow my instructions. (I had them all close their eyes so we would avoid acting out behavior.) I asked them to think of their own memory of something purple and move their body in steady slow motion (to three slow beats on the drum) to make a body shape that feels like the mood of that color. Then, I whispered 'purple' and beat the drum as they all improvised a movement. 'Great, beautiful . . . hold that position. Now go back to your starting position and move in slow motion to that purple shape again.' I had them repeat that sequence.

"Next, I added opportunities for them to create a movement to a yellow, then gray, then turquoise shape. Each time I added a new color, I asked them to think about that color and move and remember each in sequence, 'purple, yellow, gray, turquoise.' We practiced moving smoothly and beautifully from starting positions to each color in a seamless fashion. I then took the drum away and told them I wanted them to perform their 'color dance' all the way through, color to color, without stopping, and then perform it in backwards order, ending in starting position. They could move at their own pace but needed to 'make it beautiful.' The students really had to think about this! Once they practiced the dance all the way through their 'colors' and then backward back to starting position (still with their eyes closed), we were ready to perform. This was a very personalized and private choreography because there was no audience, just complete immersion into their own storyline for their color dance. It was beautiful!"

Dr. McDonald decided to extend her students' sense of story and sequence into a writing and visual art activity. She describes what happened next:

"After they danced (and they all did), I asked them to return to their seats and use the large piece of white construction paper given to them. They folded the paper into four sections. I provided crayons, markers, and watercolor paints and brushes. I asked the students to write a few sentences about their image of each color (with the writing prompt 'as purple as . . . ') and then illustrate their writing. The writing and illustrations were beautiful and highly creative. One student wrote, 'as yellow as . . . the sun streaming through the new spring leaves. I awoke the first morning of our camping trip and saw the yellow glow above me and all around me. I was warm and happy.' I think their ability to write and create a color story and illustrations was profoundly shaped by their creation of their movement sequence."

Another example of using movement to increase students' awareness of story and sequence finds us in the realm of classical music. *Carnival of the Animals* was written by the French composer Camille Saint-Saëns in the late 19th century. Originally written to delight the composer's grandchildren, *Carnival of the Animals* is now one of the most frequently performed pieces of orchestral music. Frequently, performances are paired with an amusing narrative limerick written by Ogden Nash. Many symphony orchestras regularly perform this piece in special concerts designed for children and families. (Check your local symphony orchestra schedule for possible performances of this piece.)

Carnival of the Animals is a series of very short pieces about an imaginative assortment of zoo animals. Sections of this piece capture the way certain animals move and communicate, such as the march of the royal lions, the apes, the tortoises, the dance of the fossils, the birds of the aviary, the kangaroos, the elephant, the aquarium, etc. Each section has a distinct sound and features certain instruments (e.g., elephants = string bass).

Several classes attended a symphony performance of *Carnival of the Animals*. Afterward, the children wanted to hear the music again. Ms. Nordall's third-grade class particularly liked the section entitled "The Aquarium." This section of the music reminded her students of an underwater scene. After listening to "The Aquarium" several times, Ms. Nordall noticed there were two themes that seemed to alternate throughout the short piece. With considerable imagination, she describes her lesson in the following way:

> "When I listened to the music over and over again, I liked it even more. I guess that's why they call it a 'classic.' I could hear two main themes in the music that seemed to alternate with each other. Because the title was 'The Aquarium,' I imagined there were two main characters in the 'story' of the music—colorful fish and sea plants at the bottom of the aquarium. The scene I imagined was the water flowing through a giant aquarium and the sea plants moving in a very fluid way. Then the fish began to swim through the plants. Eventually, the fish and the plants moved together as if dancing together. Then I hear a little part that sounded like bubbles rising to the surface of the tank. This happened four times. Finally, the music slowed down and I imagined the plants and the fish were resting a bit.
>
> "I shared my ideas with my students. I created a simple chart with icons of the sea plants and the fish matching their 'order' or sequence in the story of the music. I included the 'bubbles' and the slowing down at the end. The chart was very simple and effective. We then experimented with movements we could use for the sea plants and for the fish."

Ms. Nordall was surprised at the results. She added:

> "We then listened to the CD recording a few more times so that the students could identify each section. I pointed to the chart at first and then they were able to identify the parts of our 'story' without my help. My little idea had become a ballet of sorts!
>
> "One half of the class were the sea plants; one half were the fish. We experimented with how to make our movements imaginative and match the musical events. They then switched roles. I was amazed when they wanted to research more about the composer, Saint-Saëns, and perform their dance for another class. Several other teachers at my school became interested in what we were doing and now we have plans to create choreography and original narration for the entire *Carnival of the Animals*."

Ms. Nordall's willingness to experiment with movement caused her students to become involved with a musical storyline sequence in a nonverbal way. They were allowed the freedom to move and create their own imaginative interactions with that story. Their active involvement in the sequence of the music etched that music in their memory. One student commented, "I want to learn about more composers and music that has a story."

PHONEMIC AWARENESS AND PHONICS

As we have noted in this book as well as in this chapter, we want our students to read and understand what they are reading. At the most basic level, to understand what they are reading, students must be able to decode words. While phonemic awareness is often considered the responsibility of early childhood educators, work on phonics, spelling, and word study extends well into the elementary and middle school years.

One of the ways that we can extend our students' understanding of the ways in which letters and words work is to have them make words. Making words is an instruction strategy in which students manipulate letters to create words (Cunningham, 1994). Typically students are provided a series of letters on small pieces of paper that they can use to create a series of words. The selected letters can all be used to create one big word. Figure 5.3 is a photograph of a typical making words letter-stand for the word *monster.*

FIGURE 5.3. Making words.

While the typical making words activity involves movement and manipulatives (small objects students can maneuver with their hands) as students select and change letters to create words, Mr. Fisher wanted to increase the amount of movement for a group of second graders.

Instead of providing each student with small pieces of paper with the letters written on them, he created necklaces with string and construction paper for the letters. On one particular day, eight students stood in the front of the classroom with letters around their necks: *a, d, r, n, o, i, s, u.*

Students who were not wearing letters, but who had small dry-erase boards at their desks were invited to write down one-letter words. They wrote *a* and *I*. Then came two-letter words, and they wrote *no, is, an, do,* etc. As students were selected to identify words, the students with the letters around their necks moved to create the word that was spelled. As they moved to three-letter words, students found *don, nor, sun,* and a host of other words in the pile of letters. Again, the students with the letters around their necks moved to spell out the words that their peers at their desks identified.

Pausing on the word *sun,* Mr. Fisher asked the class to look at that word again and think of a way to send one letter back to the letter pile and bring a new letter up to make a new word. Jessica sent the *u* back and brought the *o* forward to make *son.* Mr. Fisher asked if they could do it again. Anthony sent the *s* back and brought the *r* up to make *Ron.* From there, they created *run, ran, rad, sad, sud,* and so on. These letter-substitution activities are critical for students' understanding of phonics and spelling.

As they progressed through their making words lesson, students found the following words: *ruin, ruins, rain, round, around, drain,* and a number of other words. When it came time to use all of the letters, Michael was jumping up excitedly. When called on, he identified *dinosaur* as the big word. At that time, Mr. Fisher started a CD with the recording of "The Dinosaur Dance." At specific points, students are invited to "raise their dinosaur knee, shake their dinosaur toes, touch their dinosaur nose," and so on. Through movement and a specific focus on letters and words, these students will become proficient users of the language.

BACKGROUND KNOWLEDGE AND VOCABULARY

How many words does a person need to know to be successful? That question has been asked for decades. By the time a student reaches high school, it has been estimated that he or she will need to know at least 85,000 word families that comprise more than 500,000 words. Yikes! That's a lot of words and ideas to teach. Thankfully, students learn a lot of words as they read. Other words they need to be taught.

Ms. Allen wanted her fifth-grade students to use science and math vocabulary in a creative, active, and interactive way. She designed an activity based on the traditional pantomime activity "statues." Ms. Allen asked her students to imagine a snowy day. (This is a stretch because she lives in San Diego, California!) She then divided her students into two groups: "snowpeople" and "builders." The snowpeople were asked to sit on the floor and make themselves into a ball. The builders were to come to the front of the room and read a secret word (not to be shared with the snowpeople). This secret word (written on large cards) was shown to the builders. Some of the cards included the following words: desert animals, amphibians, marsupials, parallelograms, bacteria, pentagons, symmetrical, asymmetrical, etc. The builders' job was to return to their snowperson and silently shape their "snow" into a frozen sculpture based on that secret word. The snowpeople had to hold that body shape.

When finished building, the builders then returned to the front of the room, faced their snowpeople and announced, "We built a room full of _____, who melt." The snowpeople would then slowly melt down to the floor. Then the students switched roles, and the new builders came to Ms. Allen for a new secret word. They played this movement game many times, and as a result covered the entire new vocabulary list in science and math!

Dr. McDonald wanted her inner-city middle school students to know and understand more background and vocabulary about the American revolutionary era. She also wanted them to learn some traditional American songs and knew that the song "Yankee Doodle Dandy" would be a favorite. After she taught them the song, the students were introduced to the background and meaning of this historical song text. Using the source books *Songs Sung Red, White, and Blue: The Stories Behind America's Best-Loved Patriotic Songs* (Collins, 2003) and *From Sea to Shining Sea: A Treasury of American Folklore and Folk Songs* (Cohn, 1993), Dr. McDonald created the Readers' Theatre script found in Figure 5.4.

After singing the song and performing the Readers' Theatre, Dr. McDonald's middle school class created a simple circle dance to go with the song. Her students researched the traditional clothing and hats of the patriot army and added their own costumes. They performed the Yankee Doodle Readers' Theatre, song, and dance for classes at the elementary school. One of the middle school students commented, "Can we learn songs and dances about the Civil War?"

Reader #1: Songs have a history and their words tell an ever-changing story. Today, Americans are known as "Yankees" all over the world and our song "Yankee Doodle Dandy" is sung, played, and enjoyed by people everywhere.

Reader #2: The song "Yankee Doodle" has a long and very funny history. It has been popular in America and around the world for more than 200 years. The original tune was heard in England in the 1600s and was originally known as "Nancy Dawson." Then the song took on new forms and became known as "Nankey Doodle."

Reader #3: A "Nankey" was a Puritan, a member of a group of people who questioned and rejected traditional British government and religious establishments. The song makes fun of these people as slow and simple-minded. Puritans, as we know, eventually settled in America at Plymouth Rock and beyond, so the tradition of making fun of them continued during colonial times. Little did anyone know what would happen to this song and a nation about to be born.

Reader #4: There is a popular legend that when the Native Americans first met the Puritan settlers they had trouble pronouncing the word "English." Instead, the natives used the slang word "Nankey" in referring to the Puritan settlers but actually pronounced the word as "Yankee." So, eventually the British began to sing the words "Yankee Doodle" instead. The story goes on . . .

Reader #5: The man who wrote the words we know today was Dr. Richard Shuckburgh, a surgeon in the British Army stationed in the American colonies during the Revolutionary War. He wrote the words to "Yankee Doodle" to make fun of the poor American troops, their ragged clothes, carefree attitudes, disorganization, and lack of traditional British military discipline and training.

Reader #6: The words "thick as hasty pudding" actually meant the American soldiers were very disorganized and slow. A "dandy" was a person who acted more important than he really was, and the American soldiers were said to be more interested in dancing, music, and fun than the British soldiers of the time.

Reader #7: Captain Washington (George Washington) seemed to be giving a few too many orders to his men. . . . "I guess there was a million." We all know that in another popular version of the song, someone seemed have had a pony named "Macaroni," which seems to be pretty close to our slang for "noodle brained"! A "macaroni" was actually a knot located around a hat brim where people placed a feather.

Reader #8: The Americans surprised the British and adopted the song "Yankee Doodle" as their very own. The song became a source of great Colonial pride. They loved the humor and the tune so much, they ended up singing, marching, whistling, and playing the fife and drum to "Yankee Doodle" wherever they went.

Reader #9: In fact, when the British troops surrendered, the British general, Lord Cornwallis, paraded his well-dressed troops to meet the American general, George Washington. Thousands of Americans looked on. When Lord Cornwallis handed over his sword (a signal of official surrender), George Washington gave a signal. The American band began playing "Yankee Doodle" as loudly as they could.

Reader #10: We wonder if it was the Americans' way of making fun of the British right back by actually enjoying and adopting a song meant to make fun of them. Maybe that's the best thing to do when people make fun of us!

FIGURE 5.4. Readers' Theatre script.

From *Teaching Literacy through the Arts* by Nan L. McDonald and Douglas Fisher. Copyright 2006 by The Guilford Press. Permission to photocopy this figure is granted to purchasers of this book for personal use only. See copyright page for details.

FLUENCY

Readers' Theatre can provide students with interesting and dramatic contexts to increase fluency. Children's books with poetic text containing a recurring section or refrain can be ideal for creating a poetic Readers' Theatre. Students can learn or create a group movement to the words of the recurring section and then work in small groups to create different movements for each verse.

Ms. Nguyen was interested in designing a Readers' Theatre using the book *Where Do Falling Stars Go?* by Melanie Friedersdorf (1997). The recurring refrain in this book is "Where do falling stars go? Do you know? Do you know?" This refrain alternates with charming poetic verse, all in question format (e.g., "Do they drop in a big, black hole? Or do they stop and roll and roll? Do they land in rover's dish? Do they turn into starfish?" Ms. Nguyen typed out the text of the book and labeled the refrain and verses. She taught her class a simple group movement on the refrain and placed students in small groups according to where they were sitting in the classroom. (She wanted to make things simple and have students stay in their usual seats and work with peers nearby.) The groups were told to create a movement they could perform seated at their desks as they read aloud their verse.

Ms. Nguyen describes what happened next:

> "I wasn't prepared for all the excitement. My students immediately read their verses over and over again and practiced new movement ideas as they did so. Some decided to read their verse loudly, some whispered, depending on the words and movements of the verse. They even added facial expression to their movements. It only took my students about 4 minutes to come up with their idea, which I asked them to practice for our class 'performance.'
>
> "Our 'performance' mode caused my students really to be interested in doing their best out-loud reading. When every group seemed ready, I asked the students to focus and get ready for the performance. I also suggested that they check their 'script' to follow along and know when it was their verse. We started at the beginning with the first 'Where do falling stars go? Do you know? Do you know?' refrain with movement. Then the first verse group performed, then the large group refrain, and so forth. We didn't stop to applaud each group, but kept the rhythm of the text and movements going. At the end, the students broke into spontaneous applause. I can tell you this is the first time I've heard applause during literacy instruction! I am rethinking how to use movement more on a daily basis."

The students in this example were able to master the tasks of reading aloud and moving to one verse of a larger work. They were able to do so in a short period of time. Movement cemented the meaning and rhythm of the text. Students' partic-ipation in the recurring refrain sections kept everyone alert and involved. Atten-tion could not wander. Also, the students were very excited to see and hear their peers' ideas on verses very different from their own.

There are many children's books with interesting song texts and CD record-ings (see Figure 5.5). Movement can easily be added to these texts and music to improve students' reading fluency. Both the music and movement challenge stu-dents to master words more quickly because to do so will allow a student to partic-ipate in an engaging group experience. Simply put, students will want to read aloud because it is fun!

Mr. McFarlane wanted his students to learn more about the human skeletal system. He knew his students could find information in their science texts, but their out-loud reading from this text was dry and uninvolved. Mr. McFarlane attended a state reading conference and found the book *Dem Bones* by Bob Barner (1996). The text of this book is the well-known African American spiritual by the same title. Mr. McFarlane learned this song as a child and thought his students might love it too.

Each page of *Dem Bones* features Barner's delightful illustrations of dancing skeletons playing various instruments and pointing to or featuring the "bone" of that part of the song text (e.g., "Ankle bone connected to da leg bone."). The book also has a page at the end with a skeleton labeled with the scientific names for each bone mentioned in the song text. Mr. McFarlane also noticed that each page of *Dem Bones* had a short, amusing paragraph about a bone of the body. For example:

LEG BONE

The leg bone is actually two bones, the tibia and the fibula. The fibula, the smaller of the two, is located on the little toe side of your leg. You can feel the tibia at the front of your lower leg. It's the one that really hurts if you get kicked in the shin!

Archambault, J., & Martin, B. (1989). *Chicka chicka boom boom.* New York: Scholastic.
Barnwell, Y. (1998). *No mirrors in my nana's house.* Orlando, FL: Harcourt Brace.
Chapin-Carpenter, M. (1998). *Halley came to Jackson.* New York: HarperCollins.
Gatti, A. (1997). *The magic flute.* San Francisco: Chronicle Books.
Gollub, M. (2000). *The jazz fly.* Santa Rosa, CA: Tortuga Press.
Guthrie, W. (2000). *Howdi do.* Cambridge, MA: Candlewick.
Judd, N. (1999). *Love can build a bridge.* New York: HarperCollins.
Troupe, Q. (2005). *Little Stevie Wonder.* New York: Houghton Mifflin.

FIGURE 5.5. Books that come with recordings.

Mr. McFarlane describes his lesson activity as follows:

"I searched the Web for versions of the song 'Dem Bones' (or 'Dry Bones') I located two versions and purchased them from the Apple Music Store online. One recording is more traditional, followed by a rap version that starts in a reverse order from the head bone down to the foot bone! Although the words in the book vary a little bit from the recording, that's okay.

"I started by playing the CD recording and showing the book to my students. They started singing along almost immediately. I then assigned tasks to my class. One group, 'scientists,' was in charge of reading aloud all the narrative facts about the bones. (I typed these out on notecards, so each student in that group could have their own part.) Another group made up movements to each verse and were to be 'singers and dancers.' Another group, 'skeletons,' made up a group dance we could all do at the beginning part of the music and at the end. This group added percussion instruments to sound like bones dancing!

"After about 15 minutes, we put everything together. The scientists decided to draw a giant skeleton and label the bones with the common word and the scientific word to point to during their part of our performance. Our performance had us all doing the skeleton dance group's idea at the beginning, then immediately after each verse was sung and moved by our singers/dancers, I paused the CD so our scientists could read their fact paragraph out loud, then the CD continued and the same pattern of activity happened on each verse. We ended with an amazing skeleton dance."

Mr. McFarlane commented on the students' use of fluency:

"This activity was immediately appealing to my students. The students sang and danced, read and listened. They were up and out of their seats. They really tuned in to the scientific facts, as they were set within an interesting context. More learning took place about the human skeletal system in this one lesson than in 2 weeks of textbook activity. One student commented, 'I want to be a scientist next time!' "

COMPREHENSION

When students put all of their reading skills and processes together, they comprehend. It isn't an easy task; making sense of complex texts requires that students simultaneously mobilize a number of skills. Fortunately, the arts help students comprehend.

Dr. McDonald's students had been reading about the Underground Railroad. She wanted her students to learn the song "Follow the Drinkin' Gourd," which was sung by slaves to alert others to be ready to escape north to freedom. She found the song within a basal music text series. The song contains many bits of important information for the travelers such as, "The old man is a-waitin' for to carry you to freedom" (Harriet Tubman, who led the escaped slaves along the dangerous route, was known as "Moses" or the "Old Man") and "Dead trees will show you the way" (moss grows on the north side of trees, so the escapees could always find their way north).

Dr. McDonald's students first read aloud the text to the song. Each of the code words was discussed. The students learned that the "drinkin' gourd" was a reference to the Big Dipper constellation. Slaves used hollowed-out drinking gourds to quench their thirst. If they looked for a constellation shaped like a drinking gourd, they would find a star on the upper part of the "gourd" that pointed to the bright North Star, Polaris. The slaves only needed to follow that star to make their way north to freedom.

Dr. McDonald describes how movement was used as a catalyst to increase her students' comprehension of the song:

"I knew that the Big Dipper had a handle and a dipper in its shape. I drew a big dipper on the board and traced that shape with my arm as I said the words 'follow the drinkin' gourd.' Then, when we sung the tune and moved our arms to trace the shape, we discovered the notes exactly follow the shape of the Big Dipper outline. That movement (arm extended above our heads, as if looking to the stars and tracing the outline of the Big Dipper) kept the kids focused on the song and on the meaning of the escape north.

"We sang the song several times. Students developed movement ideas for the action of the song text. We illustrated scenes from the song and cre-

ated a class 'freedom quilt' about the secret codes within the song. (Freedom quilts were hung on the roofs of 'safe houses,' places to hide and seek shelter along the Underground Railroad.) Finally, we found a book based on this song, *Follow the Drinking Gourd* by Jeanette Winter (1988), to script as a narrated play with music and movement and performed it for other classes. We were sorry to see this unit end!"

WRITING

As our colleague from San Diego State University often reminds us, "All writers can read." Importantly, we should note that the reverse is not always true—not all readers can write. In the rush to improve reading achievement, we need to remember that writing development is a critical skill. Attention to writing instruction and writing development will ensure that all students become strong readers and thinkers.

In Appendix D, students perform haiku of the Japanese masters in three distinct ways. First, they say the haiku slowly and expressively. They then say and dramatically move to the haiku. Finally, they do movement only by "thinking the haiku" as they move. After the experience of preparing this performance, students are asked to write their own haiku. They then illustrate their haiku, create scenery, and perform their haiku with movement. Students also create a photo-essay of an original or traditional haiku and create musical compositions coordinated with the haiku movements.

The writing of original haiku is enriched by the students' direct experiences with the art form, through total body involvement. After observation and participation in this unit, one student teacher commented:

Haiku is more than poetic words on a page. It involves something much deeper than simple, profound language. The *spirit* of the author comes alive when our imaginations take hold. We were able not only to hear the words, but also to see the performers' interpretations and reactions. What a wonderful exercise to make poetry come alive! (See Appendix D)

CONCLUSION

Movement is one of many ways children learn. Children instinctively want to move and explore their world. Kinesthetic learning activities can serve to connect a child's natural way of learning to important cognitive insights about the learning at hand. In order to participate in movement and dance, students must listen, think, assimilate instructions and sequences, pattern their ideas physically, communicate and coordinate with others, become a part of a group effort, and *show* what they have learned. We can *see* their learning.

Our teacher contributors have offered very interesting, and not too complex, ways to increase literacy skills within this learning modality. We have learned that kinesthetic learning experiences do not necessarily have to be linked to polished dance performances, but rather may be used on a regular basis within our classroom instruction. As you have read, students are more than ready, willing, and able fully to engage and participate in movement and dance. In these classroom examples, students' total physical involvement served to increase their learning and participation in significant and memorable ways. Finally, teachers were both delighted and surprised at the power of these learning experiences to elicit and broaden student responses in verbal and nonverbal ways. To move *is* to learn.

STUDY QUESTIONS AND ACTIVITIES

1. Read through this chapter again and place Post-it notes near classroom examples that interest you. Mark ideas that make you think of movement and dance activity you might like to incorporate into your own literacy instruction.

2. Are there other classroom teachers at your site who use movement to increase literacy skills? At a staff or grade-level meeting, find out which classroom teachers at your school site use movement and dance (creative movement, dance to music, movement games) in their classrooms and ask them to share those ideas and resources with you.

3. Where are the dance and movement resources at your school site and community? Locate and inventory the following: books in your school library about dance and dancers, books with dance instructions and movement games, CD recordings of dance music and music appropriate for all kinds of movement, collections of songs, videos of dance around the world, teachers

and parents/grandparents with active interest and ability in dance, costumes at your school site and at students' homes, where to rent or borrow costumes and sets, where to order supplies needed, etc.

4. Make a list of three movement and dance ideas you would like to develop and use during your own literacy instruction. Discuss your ideas with an interested peer. Teach these activities and discuss the results with that peer. Did that movement activity increase students' participation and retention of literacy skills? Why or why not?

5. Find out if there are professional growth opportunities, courses, workshops, etc. involving movement and dance for the classroom teacher in your area. Visit your local dance venues, university dance departments, and dance studios to find out about student audience opportunities and educational outreach programs. One arts organization that places artists-in-residence in schools and classrooms throughout the country is Young Audiences. Go to their website (www.youngaudiences.org) to find contact information for your area. Also, see the websites listed in Resources.

REFERENCES

Barner B. (1996). *Dem bones.* San Francisco: Chronicle Books.

Cohn, A. (Ed.). (1993). *From sea to shining sea: A treasury of American folklore and folk songs.* New York: Scholastic.

Collins, A. (2003). *Songs sung red, white, and blue: The stories behind America's best-loved patriotic songs.* New York: HarperCollins.

Cornett, C. (2003). *Creating meaning through literature and the arts* (2nd ed.). Upper Saddle River, NJ: Merrill Prentice Hall.

Corso, M. (1997, April 9). *Children who desperately want to read, but are not working at grade level: Use movement patterns as "windows" to discover why.* Paper presented at the annual international conference of the Association for Children's Education, Portland, OR. (ERIC Document Reproduction Service No. CS01 660)

Cunninghan, P. (1994). *Making words: Multilevel, hands-on developmentally appropriate spelling and phonics activities grades 1–3.* Carthage, IL: Good Apple.

Friedersdorf, M. (1997). *Where do falling stars go?* Colorado Springs, CO: Peaceful Village.

Gardner, H. (1999). *The disciplined mind.* New York: Simon & Schuster.

Jensen, E. (2001). *Arts with the brain in mind.* Alexandria, VA: Association for Supervision and Curriculum Development.

Rappaport, D. (2001). *Martin's big words: The life of Dr. Martin Luther King, Jr.* New York: Jump at the Sun.

Reber, A. S. (1993). *Implicit learning and tacit knowledge: An essay on the cognitive unconscious.* New York: Oxford University Press.

Winter, J. (1988). *Follow the drinking gourd.* New York: Knopf.

CHAPTER 6
PUTTING IT ALL TOGETHER

In my classroom . . .

    . . . incorporating art in my English language learner lessons is essential. Music, drama, drawing, and singing—any of these mediums always proves engaging. They help reinforce the lesson I'm teaching. All the while, they're laughing and giggling. These activities extend my teaching to a whole other level. Last, but not least, it provides lifelong memories that will remain forever.

                                       —Norma Sandoval

CHAPTER 6 ANTICIPATION GUIDE

Before reading this chapter: A = agree D = disagree	Statements	After reading this chapter: A = agree D = disagree
	Arts activities can easily be incorporated into my own literacy instruction.	
	My efforts to infuse the arts into literacy instruction will be well received by my school site administration.	
	I have a number of arts ideas I would like to try within my literacy instruction.	

    This book has provided many excellent real-life examples of how literacy instruction can be enlivened and enhanced by and through the arts. Our classroom teacher contributors have offered invaluable insights about the intent, function, and implementation of their integrated instruction. They have also shared with us the many positive results of their classroom activities, including student commentary. Through this evidence we can draw some important conclusions:

1. The four arts (music, visual art, theater/drama, and movement/dance) can be easily and effectively integrated into literacy instruction in the general classroom.

2. Classroom teachers can successfully plan, teach, and evaluate arts activities within literacy instruction and across multiple content areas.

3. Classroom teachers cite the following effects of teaching with and through the arts: increased literacy skills, student engagement and participation, teacher satisfaction, and memory of the learning at hand.

With these results in mind, we would like to encourage you to integrate arts activities into your own literacy instruction. This chapter provides you with self-study tools to get you started. First, let's look at an example of a completed lesson pre-plan (Figure 6.1) based on a literacy through the arts lesson about Japanese haiku (see Appendix D). Here, you will see the teacher's plan for the lesson *before* the lesson was actually taught.

In the example shown in Figure 6.1, notice that the teacher has a very clear purpose in mind. She wants her students to understand the cultural context and history of the haiku genre through reading a book about the haiku master poet Issa. She eventually wants her students to internalize the meaning of a haiku text through direct and active interactions with that text. The plan is to provide opportunities for students to become directly involved with haiku through cooperative group processes using expressive oral language, movement, dramatization, and illustration purposely linked to the meaning of the haiku text. The students will perform their ideas for others. Finally, the teacher believes these multiple interactions with the meaning of haiku are important concepts for the students to obtain *before* asking them to write their own haiku poetry.

Let's now find out what happened through reading the teacher's reflection. Reflection is an important part of our professional development. However, we often don't take the time to reflect or are not provided with opportunities or encouragement to do so upon our practice individually or with peers. When teachers are able to do so upon their teaching (through writing and discussion), they are more able to process how they teach and how their students learn. They are able to consider possible solutions to teaching challenges. They are often able to implement new ideas in their classrooms and reflect again on those changes.

Now, back to what actually happened during this haiku lesson. Figure 6.2 was filled out after the haiku lesson was taught. Within this reflection, we see that the teacher learned along with her students. She accomplished her literacy goals in highly creative ways. Student participation was dramatically (no pun intended!)

Name: <u>Nan McDonald</u> Grade level/subject you teach: <u>Grade 4</u>

Fill in this chart before you teach your lesson. Fill in the second chart **after** your lesson.

Questions to consider	Your ideas here
Topic or theme?	Haiku, Japanese haiku master poet—Issa
Content area? Content area standards?	Language Arts, Social Studies *Language Arts*: Genre studies (poems), writing strategies, vocabulary development *Social Studies*: Understanding and appreciation of cultural contributions
Literacy components?	[x] oral language [ ] concepts of print [x] sense of story and sequence [ ] phonemic awareness and phonics [x] background knowledge and vocabulary [x] fluency [x] comprehension [x] writing
Which arts will be incorporated into the content area?	[x] music [x] visual arts [x] theater drama [x] movement/dance
What kind of activities within the arts will be used?	Musical listening, expressive recitation of traditional haiku, viewing of Japanese watercolor paintings, creative movement and dramatization of haiku in informal performance for others, illustration of haiku, writing of original haiku.

(continued)

FIGURE 6.1. Completed lesson idea for teaching with and through the arts.

What do I hope to accomplish in this lesson?	I hope to find a way for the study of haiku to come alive for my students. Rather than the usual dry study of numbers of lines and syllables, I want my students to get out of their chairs and move as they express the meaning of the haiku. I want them to be able to express the nuances and meaning of the haiku through oral language paired with movement. We will read a book about the haiku poet Issa (*Cool Melons—Turn to Frogs!* by Matthew Gollub, 1998, Lee and Low). They will work in small cooperative groups to read, reread, and memorize a traditional haiku. They will then explore ways to recite the poem together expressively and create movements to portray dramatically the meaning of their haiku. They will illustrate their haiku and will perform their haiku for others. My goal is to have the students internalize their haiku through total physical involvement. Finally, they will write original haiku.
How will I assess learning and literacy skill development during this integrated lesson?	By watching students' group work processes and performances, viewing their illustrations, and reading their original haiku, I should be able to assess their use of expressive oral language, comprehension of the haiku and haiku form, visualization and internalization of the haiku text meanings, etc.

FIGURE 6.1. (*continued*)

*Fill in this chart **after** you teach your lesson. Keep both charts for discussion with others.*

Name: Nan McDonald   Grade level/subject you teach: Grade 4

Step-by-step (what was actually done):

1. To set the mood, I used CD background music (Japanese flute—shakuhachi). Students silently mirrored my very slow movements, then did mirror movements with a partner, alternating leaders.
2. Music continues. . . . I silently showed pictures of Japanese watercolor paintings and then discussed the simplicity and beauty of the paintings and how Japanese poets were often also artists and musicians.
3. I modeled a dramatized haiku poem in three ways: expressive speech, expressive speech with created whole-body movements, and movements alone, "thinking" the haiku text. The students echoed my sequence and eventually did it without my lead.
4. Students formed groups of five to seven. Each group was assigned a haiku by Issa from the Gollub book. They were asked to create a three-part (see above) performance of their haiku.
5. Once the group had practiced their haiku, they could create a paper mural backdrop for their haiku performance. (This artwork took a long time and could have been done on another day!)
6. The class was gathered together and each group performed. First their artwork was held up as scenery, then the students did their haiku in three ways. I used the flute music (very low volume) during the group performances and turned the volume up as we transitioned from group to group. We held our applause until the end and hung the artwork around the classroom.
7. The next day we read aloud *Cool Melons—Turn to Frogs!* by Matthew Gollub. The students were very interested in the book as they had performed Issa's haiku found in the book. We decided to read aloud the book again and "insert" their performances of Issa's haiku when they appeared in the text! The students voted to perform the book as a Readers' Theatre with their haiku scenes for another fourth-grade class the following week!
8. The next day the students wrote original haiku (after a discussion of appropriate syllables and form), illustrated their haiku, and hung the art and poems in a haiku gallery on our classroom wall.

Materials used:

- *Cool Melons—Turn to Frogs!* by Matthew Gollub (1998, Lee and Low) (This book contains many haiku by Issa.)
- CD recording of traditional Japanese flute and koto music (harp) found online or in the world music section at music stores.
- Large butcher paper, oil or chalk pastels, crayons, marker pens, Kleenex to smear colors.
- Blown-up color copies of Japanese watercolor paintings from an art book in the school library.

How did the art(s) contribute to students' literacy development within this lesson? Circle the appropriate literacy components:

(oral language), concepts of print, (sense of story and sequence), phonemic awareness and phonics, (background knowledge and vocabulary), (fluency), (comprehension), (writing)

I can't imagine doing a lesson or unit on haiku in any other way! My students were very excited to learn about haiku, see the art, work in groups and perform for others. The haiku came to life. I imagine this was the first opportunity most of my students have had to visualize poetry by using movement, speech, and art. They were able to use oral language in an expressive and artistic way, move to the meaning of the haiku, show that they understood the form by writing their own, and increase their comprehension through performing and viewing others' performances. Incidentally, the Gollub book is now one of their favorites!

(continued)

FIGURE 6.2. Completed reflection on teaching with and through the arts.

How did it go? **Your** thoughts about the final products/projects/student learning? How did you assess student learning in this lesson?

The students learned not only about Japanese culture and haiku, but also how to work in cooperative groups to create something on demand. Students needed to use leadership skills, be willing to try something new, and perform in front of others despite any anxiety. This lesson reached all learners and caused students to synthesize their own poems to create art and vocal effects. They also used their visualization skills to make the haiku come alive on paper and in the performance. Haiku is more than poetic words on a page. It involves something much deeper than simple, profound language. The spirit of the author comes alive when our imaginations take hold. We were able not only to hear the words, but also to see the performers' interpretations and reactions. What a wonderful exercise to make poetry come alive!

Quotes from **students** about this lesson:

From a grade 4 student: "We made the haiku come alive with what we saw in the poem."
From a student teacher: "The words floated through the bodies of others like the haiku's spell had taken over them. I could see the words moving and taking shape before me."

Changes to consider for the next time you teach this lesson:

This idea became a 3- to 5-day lesson unit! Day 1 could be the haiku practice in groups. Day 2 could be the illustrations. Day 3 could be another practice, the group performances, and the read-aloud of Gollub's book. Day 4 could be the writing of the original student haiku and illustrations. Finally, the Gollub book Readers' Theatre and haiku scenes could be performed for another class on another day. Now I know how long it takes for students to work in groups and illustrate! Artwork takes at least 30 to 45 minutes. The artwork was fascinating to the students. They all wanted to take their time to make their scenery capture the meaning of their group haiku. Oil pastels are VERY messy, so the kids need to wear old shirts!

The performance of the Gollub book and group haiku scenes was especially beautiful and an excellent end-product for our haiku unit. The students guided other fourth graders through our haiku gallery and read their original haiku to others. Many other teachers were inspired to teach this unit.

Things to consider for my next integrated arts lesson:

Simplify a bit. Allow for more art time. Teach in stages and let learning build upon learning and sink in over time. It is very important to reward my students for all progress, even if end-products are not perfect. We did a good job of not making this a competitive experience (à la Star Search!) for the students and praised all efforts. I need to remember how powerful the arts are and how they increase student motivation, participation, and expression. It was well worth the creative effort.

FIGURE 6.2. (continued)

affected by the arts activities, and enthusiasm about learning about haiku was greatly enhanced. Her class was so excited about their haiku experience, they wanted to perform what they had learned for others. Finally, both teacher and students were left with a meaningful and powerful memory of their haiku study. Isn't this what we would all like to achieve within our literacy instruction?

We hope you will consider the following steps as you plan and implement arts activities within your literacy instruction.

1. Select one theme or topic within your literacy instruction that you would like to develop with and through the arts.

2. Identify language arts content standards to be used in your lesson.

3. Identify literacy components your students need to develop.

4. Fill out Figure 6.3 (pp. 109–110).

5. Identify materials you'll need. Refer to the extensive resource list at the end of this chapter. Identify sources of materials at your school's site and elsewhere.

6. Discuss your idea with a teaching peer or arts specialist at your school site. Solicit their ideas and input.

7. Teach your lesson.

8. Fill in Figure 6.4 (pp. 111–112) soon after your lesson to reflect upon your successes and plans for revision.

9. Discuss your reflection form (completed Figure 6.4) with a teaching peer.

10. Create a notebook or file of your lesson plans and reflections. Talk to other teachers about what you have taught. Share a lesson idea at a grade-level meeting.

*   *   *

It has been our distinct pleasure to share the stories of many classroom teachers who have committed their creative energies to teaching with and through the arts. By doing so, their classroom literacy instruction has been measurably enhanced. Their students' literacy skills have been increased in powerful and significant ways. These fine professionals continue to be an example of the best our profession has to offer. They are educators involved in thinking, planning, teaching, and reflection with and for others. Together we can do amazing things toward the goal of increasing literacy skills in all our students.

Name: _____ Grade level/subject you teach: _____

Fill in this chart before you teach your lesson. Fill in the second chart **after** your lesson.

Questions to consider	Your ideas here
Topic or theme?	
Content area? Content area standards?	
Literacy components?	[ ] oral language [ ] concepts of print [ ] sense of story and sequence [ ] phonemic awareness and phonics [ ] background knowledge and vocabulary [ ] fluency [ ] comprehension [ ] writing
Which arts will be incorporated into the content area?	[ ] music [ ] visual arts [ ] theater drama [ ] movement/dance
What kind of activities within the arts will be used?	

FIGURE 6.3. Lesson idea for teaching with and through the arts (*page 1 of 2*).

What do I hope to accomplish in this lesson?	
How will I assess learning and literacy skill development during this integrated lesson?	

FIGURE 6.3. *(page 2 of 2)*

*Fill in this chart **after** you teach your lesson. Keep both charts for discussion with others.*

Name: _____ Grade level/subject you teach: _____

Step-by-step (what was actually done):
Materials used:
How did the art(s) contribute to students' literacy development within this lesson? Circle the appropriate literacy components:
oral language, concepts of print, sense of story and sequence, phonemic awareness and phonics, background knowledge and vocabulary, fluency, comprehension, writing

FIGURE 6.4. Reflection on teaching with and through the arts (*page 1 of 2*).

How did it go? **Your** thoughts about the final products/projects/student learning? How did you assess student learning in this lesson?

Quotes from **students** about this lesson:

Changes to consider for the next time you teach this lesson:

Things to consider for my next integrated arts lesson:

FIGURE 6.4. *(page 2 of 2)*

RESOURCES

VISUAL ART

For Children

Learning to Look at Art

Brown, R. (1982). *If at first you do not see.* New York: Henry Holt.

Carle, E. (1984). *The mixed-up chameleon.* New York: HarperCollins.

Carle, E. (1992). *Draw me a star.* New York: Philomel.

Carroll, C. (1996). *How artists see.* New York: Abbeville. (Series of books, each linking art to various themes: animals, artists, cities, the elements, families, feelings, people, play, work, seasons, universe)

Collins, P. (1992). *I am an artist.* Brookfield, CT: Millbrook Press.

Lionni, L. (1995). *Matthew's dream.* New York: Knopf.

Rockwell, N. (1967, 1994). *Willie was different: A children's story by Norman Rockwell.* New York: Dragonfly Books by Alfred A. Knopf.

Wolfe, G. (1999). *Oxford first book of art.* New York: Oxford University Press.

What Is Art? What Do Artists Do? Concepts, Elements, and Tools Artists Use

DePaola, T. (1989). *The art lesson.* New York: Putnam & Grosset.

Gibbons, G. (2000). *The art box.* New York: Holiday House.

Heller, R. (1995). *Color.* New York: Puffin Books.

Rylant, C. (1988). *All I see.* New York: Orchard Books.

Lives and Works of Great Painters

Anholt, L. (1994). *Camille and the sunflowers: A story about Vincent van Gogh*. New York: Barrons.

Armstrong, C. (1995). *My Monet art museum*. New York: Philomel.

Bjork, C. (1985). *Linnea in Monet's garden*. New York: R & S Books.

Boutan, M. (1995). *Monet: Art activity pack*. New York: Chronicle Books.

Boutan, M. (1996). *Matisse: Art activity pack*. New York: Chronicle Books.

Brust, B. (1994). *The amazing paper cuttings of Hans Christian Andersen*. New York: Tickner & Fields.

Flux, P. (2002). *Henri Matisse*. Chicago, IL: Reed.

Hopler, B. (1998). *Marc Chagall*. New York: Prestel-Verlag.

Isom, J. (1997). *The first starry night*. Watertown, MA: Charlesbridge.

Johnson, K., & O'Connor, J. (2002). *Henri Matisse: Drawing with scissors*. New York: Grosset & Dunlap.

Le Tord, B. (1999). *A bird or two: A story about Henri Matisse*. Grand Rapids, MI: Eerdmans Books.

Littlesugar, A. (1999). *Marie in fourth position: The story of Degas' "The Little Dancer."* New York: Paperstar.

Merberg, J., & Bober, S. (2002). *A magical day with Matisse*. San Francisco: Chronicle.

Ringgold, F., Feeman, L., & Roucher, N. (1996). *Talking to Faith Ringgold*. New York: Crown.

Sellier, M. (1996). *Chagall from A to Z*. New York: Bedrick Books.

Venezia, M. (1994–2001). *Getting to know the world's greatest artists*. New York: Children's Press. (A series that includes: Frida Kahlo, Grant Wood, Andy Warhol, El Greco, Edward Hopper, Francisco de Goya, Pieter Brueghel, Marc Chagall, Paul Klee, Henri de Toulouse-Lautrec, Paul Gauguin, Paul Cézanne, Henri Matisse, Pierre-Auguste Renoir, Claude Monet, Pablo Picasso, Salvador Dali, Norman Rockwell, Diego Rivera, Michelangelo, Dorothea Lange, Mary Cassatt, Rembrandt van Rijn, Georgia O'Keefe, Vincent van Gogh, Jackson Pollock, Alexander Calder, Leonardo da Vinci, Raphael, Sandro Botticelli, and Edgar Degas)

Welton, J. (2002). *Henri Matisse: Artists in their time*. New York: Franklin Watts.

For Teachers

Brady, M. (1997). *Dancing hearts: Creative arts with books kids love*. Golden, CO: Fulcrum Publishing.

Chambers, J., & Hood, M. (1999). *Art for writing: Creative ideas to stimulate written activities*. UK: Belair.

Cornett, C. (2003). *Creating meaning through literature and the arts: An integration resource for classroom teachers* (2nd ed.). Upper Saddle River, NJ: Merrill Prentice Hall.

Frohardt, D. (1999). *Teaching art with books kids love: Teaching art appreciation, elements of art, and principles of design with award-winning children's books*. Golden, CO: Fulcrum.

Kohl, M., & Solga, K. (1996). *Discovering great artists: Hands-on art for children in the styles of the great masters*. Bellingham, WA: Bright Ring Publishing.

Sterling, M. (1994). *Focus on artists*. Huntington Beach, CA: Teacher Created Materials.

MUSIC

Song Texts

Birdseye, T., & Birdseye, G. (1994). *She'll be comin' round the mountain*. New York: Holiday House.

Catalano, D. (1998). *Frog went a-courting: A musical play in six acts*. Honesdale, PA: Boyds Mills.

Conrad, P. (1985). *Prairie songs*. New York: HarperCollins.

Manson, C. (1993). *Over the river and through the wood*. New York: North-South Books.

Mattox, C. (1989). *Shake it to the one that you love the best: Play songs and lullabies from black musical traditions*. Nashville, TN: JTG.

McGill, A. (2000). *In the hollow of your hand: Slave lullabies*. Boston: Houghton Mifflin.

Milnes, G. (1990). *Granny will your dog bite and other mountain rhymes*. New York: Knopf.

Raschka, C. (1998). *Simple gifts*. New York: Holt.

Saport, L. (1999). *All the pretty little horses: A traditional lullaby*. New York: Clarion Books.

Spier, P. (1970). *The Erie Canal*. New York: Doubleday.

Taback, S. (1999). *Joseph had a little overcoat*. New York: Viking.

Weiss, G., & Thiele, B. (1967). *What a wonderful world*. Littleton, MA: Sundance.

Westcott, N. (1989). *Skip to my Lou*. Boston: Little, Brown.

Winter, J. (1988). *Follow the drinking gourd*. New York: Knopf

Yolen, J. (1992). *Street rhymes around the world*. Honesdale, PA: Boyds Mills Press.

Poetry and Rhythmic Text (Music and Movement)

Hopkins, L. (1997). *Song and dance*. New York: Simon & Schuster.

Igus, T. (1998). *I see the rhythm*. San Francisco: Children's Book Press.

Jabar, C. (1992). *Shimmy shake earthquake: Don't forget to dance poems*. Boston: Little, Brown.

Shields, C., & Junakovic, S. (2000). *Music*. New York: Handprint Books.

Learning to Listen to Music

Deetlefs, R. (1999). *The song of six birds*. New York: Dutton Children's Books.

Ganeri, A. (1996). *The young person's guide to the orchestra: Benjamin Britten's composition on CD narrated by Ben Kingsley*. San Diego, CA: Harcourt Brace.

Gollub, M. (2000). *The jazz fly*. Santa Rosa, CA: Tortuga Press.

Kuskin, K. (1982). *The philharmonic gets dressed*. New York: Harper & Row.

Levine, R. (2000). *Story of the orchestra: A child's introduction to the instruments, the music, the musicians and composers*. New York: Black Dog & Leventhal.

Shaik, F. (1998). *The jazz of our street*. New York: Dial.

Weatherford, C. (2000). *The sound that jazz makes*. New York: Walter and Company.

Lives and Works of Composers

Celenza, A. (2000). *The farewell symphony*. Watertown, MA: Charlesbridge.

Downing, J. (1994). *Mozart tonight*. New York: Aladdin.

Fisher, L. (1996). *William Tell*. New York: Farrar, Straus and Giroux.

Gatti, A. (1997). *The magic flute*. San Francisco: Chronicle Books.

Isadora, R. (1994). *Firebird*. New York: Putnam.

Krull, K. (1993). *Lives of the musicians: Good times, bad times (and what the neighbors thought)*. San Diego, CA: Harcourt Brace.

Pinkney, A. D. (1998). *Duke Ellington: The piano prince and his orchestra*. New York: Hyperion Books.

Press, D. (1994). *A multicultural portrait of America's music*. New York: Marshall Cavendish.

Price, L. (1990). *Aida*. San Diego, CA: Harcourt Brace.

Vernon, R. (1997). *Introducing Stravinsky*. Parsippany, NJ: Silver Burdett Press.

Vigna, G. (1999). *Masters of music: Jazz and its history*. New York: Barron's.

Instruments, Singers, and Music Making

Ardley, N. (2000). *Eyewitness books: Music: Discover the world of musical sound and the amazing variety of instruments that create music*. New York: Dorling Kindersley.

Burleigh, R. (2001). *Lookin' for bird in the big city*. New York: Harcourt.

Clement, C. (1989). *The voice of the wood*. New York: Dial.

Curtis, G. (1998). *The bat boy and his violin*. New York: Simon and Schuster.

Cutler, J. (1999). *The cello of Mr. O*. New York: Dutton.

Dengler, M. (1999). *Fiddlin' Sam*. Flagstaff, AZ: Rising Moon.

Grifalconi, A. (1999). *Tiny's hat*. New York: HarperCollins.

Hopkinson, D. (1999). *A band of angels: A story inspired by the Jubilee Singers*. New York: Atheneum.

Isadora, R. (1979). *Ben's trumpet*. New York: Greenwillow.

Johnson, A. (1996). *Picker McClikker*. Nashville, TN: Premium Press.

Lacapa, M. (1990). *The flute player: An Apache folktale*. Flagstaff, AZ: Northland.

London, J. (1993). *Hip cat*. San Francisco: Chronicle Books.

McKee, D. (1991). *The sad story of Veronica who played the violin*. New York: Kane, Miller.

McPhail, D. (1999). *Mole music*. New York: Holt.

Meyrich, C. (1989). *The musical life of Gustav Mole*. New York: Child's Play International.

Moss, L. (1995). *Zin! Zin! Zin! A violin*. New York: Simon & Schuster.

Schroeder, A. (1996). *Satchmo's blues*. New York: Doubleday.

Turner, B. (1996). *The living violin*. New York: Knopf.

DRAMA/THEATER

For Children

Aardema, V. (1975). *Why mosquitoes buzz in people's ears.* New York: Dial.

Adolf, A. (1981). *Outside/inside poems.* New York: Lothrop, Lee & Shepard.

Bemelmens, L. (1939). *Madeline.* New York: Viking Penguin.

Berger, B. (1984). *Grandfather twilight.* New York: Philomel.

Bunting, E. (1992). *The wall.* New York: Clarion.

Carle, E. (1969). *The very hungry caterpillar.* New York: Philomel.

DePaola, T. (1979). *Charlie needs a cloak.* Upper Saddle River, NJ: Prentice Hall.

Giff, P. (1980). *Today was a terrible day.* New York: Penguin.

Grimm, J. (1978). *The twelve dancing princesses.* New York: Viking.

Guarino, D. (1991). *Is your mama a llama?* New York: Scholastic.

Howard, E. (1991). *Aunt Flossie's hats (and crab cakes later).* Boston: Houghton Mifflin.

Jennings, C. A., & Harris, A. (1981). *Plays children love: A treasury of contemporary and classic plays for children.* Garden City, NY: Doubleday.

Kamerman, C. (1996). *Big book of skits: 36 short plays for young actors.* Boston: Plays.

Keats, E. (1962). *The snowy day.* New York: Viking.

Kuskin, K. (1982). *The philharmonic gets dressed.* New York: Harper & Row.

McCully, E. A. (1992). *Mirette on the high wire.* New York: Putnam.

McDermott, B. (1976). *The Golem: A Jewish legend.* Philadelphia: Lippincott.

McDermott, G. (1975). *The stonecutter.* New York: Viking.

Parish, P. (1963). *Amelia Bedelia.* New York: Harper & Row.

Sciezka, J. (1989). *The true story of the 3 little pigs by A. Wolf.* New York: Viking.

Steptoe, J. (1987). *Mufaro's beautiful daughters.* New York: Lothrop, Lee & Shepard.

Thayer, E. W. (1988). *Casey at the bat.* Boston: Godine.

Young, E. (1989). *Lon Po Po: A Red-Riding Hood story from China.* New York: Philomel.

For Teachers

Barchers, S. (1993). *Reader's Theatre for beginning readers.* Englewood, CO: Teacher Ideas.

Bray, E. (1995). *Playbuilding: A guide for group creation of plays with young people.* Portsmouth, NH: Heinemann.

Caruso, S., & Kosoff, S. (1998). *The young actor's book of improvisation: Dramatic situations from Shakespeare to Spielberg,* Vol.1. Portsmouth, NH: Heinemann.

Cornett, C. (2003). *Creating meaning through literature and the arts: An integration resource for classroom teachers* (2nd ed.). Upper Saddle River, NJ: Merrill Prentice Hall.

Heinig, R. (1993). *Creative drama for the classroom teacher.* Upper Saddle River, NJ: Merrill Prentice Hall.

Kohl, M. (1999). *Making make-believe: Fun props, costumes and creative play ideas.* Beltsville, MD: Gryphon House.

Laughlin, M., & Latrobe, K. (1990). *Reader's theatre for children.* Englewood, CO: Teacher Ideas.

Martinez, M. (1993, May). Motivating dramatic story reenactments. *The Reading Teacher, 46,* 682–688.

McCaslin, N. (1990). *Creative drama in the classroom* (5th ed.). New York: Longman.

Rosenberg, H. (1987). *Creative drama and imagination: Transforming ideas into action.* New York: Rinehart & Winston.

Ross, E., & Roe, B. (1997). Creative drama builds proficiency in reading. *The Reading Teacher, 30,* 383–387.

Spolin, V. (1996). *Theater games for the classroom: A teacher's handbook.* Evanston, IL: Northwestern University Press.

Wolf, A. (1993). *It's show time! Poetry from the page to the stage.* Asheville, NC: Poetry Alive!

Zimmerman, S. (2004). *More theatre games for young performers: Improvisation and exercises for developing acting skills.* Colorado Springs, CO: Meriwether.

DANCE

For Children

Ackerman, K., & Gammell, S. (1988). *Song and dance man.* New York: Knopf.

Ancona, G. (1998). *Let's dance!* New York: HarperCollins.

Baylor, B. (1978). *Sometimes I dance mountains.* New York: Scribner.

Evans, R. (1999). *The dance.* New York: Simon & Schuster.

Gray, L. M. (1995). *My Mama had a dancing heart.* New York: Orchard.

Jonas. A. (1989). *Color dance.* New York: Greenwillow.

Landry, A. (1964). *Come dance with me.* New York: Heinemann.

London, J. (2001). *Sun dance, water dance.* New York: Dutton.

Medearis, A. S. (1991). *Dancing with the Indians.* New York: Holiday House.

Noll, S. (1993). *Jiggle, wiggle, prance.* New York: Puffin.

Pavlova, A. (2001). *I dreamed I was a ballerina.* New York: Atheneum.

Schick, E. (1992). *I have another language, the language is dance.* New York: Macmillan.

Schroeder, A. (1989). *Ragtime turnpie.* Boston: Little, Brown.

Schumaker, W. (1996). *Dance!* Niles, IL: Harcourt Brace Jovanovich.

Sendak, M. (1963). *Where the wild things are.* New York: Harper & Row.

Tanbini, M. (2000). *Eyewitness: Dance.* New York: DK Children.

For Teachers

Benzwie, T. (1987). *A moving experience: Dance for lovers of children and the child within.* Tucson, AZ: Zephyr Press.

Fraser, D. (2000). *Danceplay: Creative movement for very young children.* New York: New American Trade Library.

Joyce, M. (1993). *First steps in teaching creative dance to children*. New York: McGraw Hill.

Lloyd, M. (1998). *Adventures in creative movement activities: A guide for teaching* (2nd ed.). Dubuque, IA: Eddie Bower Publication Company.

Longden, S., & Taucher, W. (2005). *Making music with movement and dance*. Parsippany, NJ: Foresman.

Rooyackers, P. (1998). *101 dance games for children: Fun and creativity with movement*. Alameda, CA: Hunter House.

Rooyackers, P. (2003). *101 more dance games for children: New fun and creativity with movement*. Alameda, CA: Hunter House.

MISCELLANEOUS BOOKS FOR TEACHERS

Beall, P., & Nipp, S. (1994). *Wee-sing songbooks and CDs*. New York: Price Stern Sloan.

Brady, M. (1997). *Dancing hearts: Creative arts with books kids love*. Golden, CO: Fulcrum.

Burz, H., & Marshall, K. (1999). *Performance-based curriculum for music and the visual arts: From knowing to showing*. Thousand Oaks, CA: Sage.

California Department of Education. (1996). *Literature for the visual and performing arts: Kindergarten through grade twelve*. Sacramento, CA: Author.

Chambers, J., & Hood, M. (1999). *Art for writing: Creative ideas to stimulate written activities*. Bedfordshire, UK: Belair.

Chambers, J., Hood, M., & Peake, M. (1995). *A work of art: Creative activities inspired by famous artists*. Nashville, TN: Incentive Publications.

Cornett, C. (2003). *Creating meaning through literature and the arts: An integration resource for classroom teachers* (2nd ed.). Upper Saddle River, NJ: Merrill Prentice Hall.

Frohardt, D. (1999). *Teaching art with books kids love: Teaching art appreciation, elements of art, and principles of design with award-winning children's books*. Golden, CO: Fulcrum.

Gust, J., & McChesney, J. (1995). *Learning about cultures: Literature, celebrations, games and art activities*. Carthage, IL: Teaching and Learning Company.

Hancock, M. (2000). *A celebration of literature and response: Children, books, and teachers in K–8 classrooms*. Upper Saddle River, NJ: Prentice Hall.

Henry, S. (1999). *Kids' art works: Creating with color, design, texture and more*. Charlotte, VT: Williamson.

Hierstein, J. (1995). *Art activities from award-winning picture books*. Carthage, IL: Teaching and Learning Company.

Kohl, M., & Solga, K. (1996). *Discovering great artists: Hands-on art for children in the styles of the great masters*. Bellingham, WA: Bright Ring.

Larrick, N. (1991). *Let's do a poem! Introducing poetry through listening, singing, chanting, impromptu choral reading, body movement, dance, and dramatization*. New York: Delacort Press.

Levene, D. (1993). *Music through children's literature: Themes and variations*. Englewood, CO: Teacher Ideas Press.

Ritter, D. (1991). *Literature-based art activities: Creative art projects inspired by 45 popular children's books: Pre-K–3*. Cypress, CA: Creative Teaching Press.

Schecter, D. (1997). *Science art: Projects and activities that teach science concepts and develop process skills*. New York: Scholastic.

Sterling, M. (1994). *Focus on artists*. Huntington Beach, CA: Teacher Created Materials.

Tarlow, E. (1998). *Teaching story elements with favorite books: Creative and engaging activities to explore character, plot, setting, and theme: Grades 1–3*. New York: Scholastic.

Walther, I. (1993). *Vincent van Gogh: Vision and reality*. Germany: Taschen.

Welton, J. (1992). *Eyewitness art: Monet*. New York: Dorling Kindersley.

ARTS ORGANIZATIONS

American Alliance for Theater and Education (AATE)
7475 Wisconsin Avenue, Suite 300A
Bethesda, MD 20814
Phone: (301) 951-7977
Website: www.aate.com

Advocating for theater and education of the highest standards, the American Alliance for Theater and Education (AATE) recognizes that theater is essential in peoples' lives.

American Arts Alliance
1112 16th Street NW, Suite 400
Washington, DC 20036
Phone: (202) 207-3850
Website: www.americanartsalliance.org

Main advocate for professional nonprofit arts organizations.

Dance USA
633 E Street NW
Washington, DC 20004
Phone: (202) 628-0144
Website: www.danceusa.org

The national service organization for professional dance.

Getty Center for Education in the Arts
1875 Century Park East, No. 2300
Los Angeles, CA 90067
Phone: (213) 277-9188
Website: www.artsednet.getty/edu

Mission is to improve arts education in U.S. K–12 public schools. The Getty Center coordinates partnerships between arts education agencies and schools.

The Kennedy Center's Partnerships in Education
Kennedy Center for the Performing Arts
270 F Street NW
Washington, DC 20566
Phone: (202) 416-8000
Website: artsedge.kennedy-center.org

Coalition of organizations (nonprofit) who work in partnership to make sure the arts are present and strong within American education.

Lincoln Center Institute
Lincoln Center for the Performing Arts, Inc.
70 Lincoln Center Plaza
New York, NY 10023-6594
Phone: (212) 875-5535
Website: www.lcinstitute.org

Created to increase aesthetic education through educational partnerships with schools. Cities currently involved: Albany, Binghamton, Buffalo, New York City, Rochester, Syracuse, and Utica; Philadelphia; Wilmington, Delaware; Nashville and Memphis, Tennessee; Bowling Green, Ohio; Lincoln, Nebraska; Houston, Texas; Tulsa, Oklahoma; San Diego, California; and Melbourne, Australia.

Music Educators National Conference (MENC)
1902 Association Drive
Reston, VA 22091
Phone: (703) 860-4000
Website: www.menc.org

"Umbrella" association of more than 100,000 educators devoted to music education for all children. Promotes music in the schools and community and music education for lifelong learning. MENC developed National Standards in Music in 1994. State and regional sections of MENC are within your area. Annual and biannual conferences offer a vast array of professional development in music education. MENC has many professional publications appropriate for classroom music teaching and advocacy for music in education.

National Art Education Association (NAEA)
1916 Association Drive
Reston, VA 22091
Phone: (703) 860-8000
Website: www.arts.arizona.edu/arted/12-1-arted.html

National association (with state branches) for educators and others concerned with education in visual art. Helped develop National Standards in Visual Art.

National Dance Association
1900 Association Drive
Reston, VA 22091
Phone: (703) 476-3421
Website: www.aahperd.org/nda

   National association (with state branches) for educators and others concerned with education in dance.

National Endowment for the Arts
1100 Pennsylvania Avenue NW
Washington, DC 20506
Phone: (202) 682-5426
Website: arts.endow.gov

   Website offers information about features and news in the arts, grant opportunities, links to state and regional arts organizations, and "Arts Resource Center" of publications, national arts service organizations, and so forth.

WEBSITES

The Art Room
www.arts.ufl.edu/art/rt_room/

   Activities and resources for visual arts provided by the University of Florida.

Arts Edge
artsedge.kennedy-center.org

   Lesson plans and other resources provided by the Kennedy Center for the Arts.

Arts Resource Connection
www.mcae.k12.mn.us/art_connection/art_connection.html

   Arts education resource provided by Minnesota's Center for Arts Education.

ArtsEdNet
www.getty.edu/education/

   Extensive curriculum, lesson plans, and resources provided by the Getty Center.

Crayola Arts Education
www.crayola.com

   Teachers and others share ideas, lessons, and arts advocacy.

The Foundation Center
www.fdncenter.org

   Provides guides to grant and research writing.

International Council of Museums

www.icom.org

> Organization committed to ethical and professional museum administration.

Learning in Motion

www.learn.motion.com/

> Educational software distributor.

Storytelling, etc.

falcon.jmu.edu/~ramseyil/

> Numerous and varied links to educational literature and art websites.

Virtual Museums

www.icom.org/vlmp

> Find virtual museums from all over the globe.

World Wide Arts Resources

www.wwar.com

> More than one thousand types of resources and links to websites.

STORMY WEATHER

*Leading Purposeful Curriculum Integration
with and through the Arts*

The call for curriculum integration *with* and *through* the arts is evident within many elementary school environments. Arts specialists are frequently asked to link their classroom curriculum to other content area instructional goals and standards. Furthermore, fully one-third of national, state, and local content standards in the arts (music, dance, theater, and visual arts) stress the importance of linking arts instruction in meaningful ways to other curriculum content areas and within appropriate historical and cultural contexts (Music Educators National Conference [MENC], 1994a, 1994b). What may not be clear is how we might begin to integrate our instruction. Simply put, how do we connect learning within the general curriculum and at the same time preserve the integrity of discipline-specific instruction in the arts?

The idea we propose here is not to dilute the content of either the arts or other core subjects. Rather, it is to establish purposeful integrated learning connections designed to increase student understanding, participation, enjoyment, and knowledge through expressive avenues for learning that children's literature and the arts can and do naturally provide (Hancock, 2000; McDonald & Fisher, 2002). Furthermore, we seek to explore ways to augment children's education in the arts by increasing teacher interest and empowering educators toward the delivery of integrated instruction (McDonald & Fisher, 2002). Comprehensive instructional goals such as these require teacher leadership and collaborations of a new kind— one of listening and creating together through considerations of others' viewpoints, expertise, and contributions to broader instructional goals. We arts specialists are simply, within these new contexts, no longer a solo act.

Our purpose here is to offer a direct example of one integrated curriculum collaboration led by an elementary general music teacher with his general classroom teacher colleagues. This 3-week, integrated unit offers direct teaching examples and ideas for shared performance featuring the arts in connection with learning in science, social studies, and language arts.

STORM CLOUDS ARE GATHERING

Scenario: On a typical day at an urban elementary school, a primary classroom teacher initiated her expected daily "weather check" with her students. As they do every day, the students scrambled to line up, go outside the classroom, look up quickly at the morning sky, and answer the standard question "What's the weather like today?" They knew they needed to answer with a simple, prescribed menu of one-word descriptors: sunny, cloudy, rainy, or stormy. However, today in this class Anthony answered, "Feels like a storm is comin' where everything gets really quiet and then you can count the seconds between the crackle lightning and the thunder booms. My grandma told me to count so I could know that the longer it took, that's how far away the lightning is. I still get scared anyway, even if I get to 10."

The teacher swiftly turned the class's attention to the rest of her science lesson. Yet, Anthony's enthusiastic and observant weather comment began to haunt her. Later, this teacher commented to her friend, the school music teacher, "I get so frustrated with the limitations of our routine 'weather check.' I know our study of weather changes has to be more interesting to the kids and to me. I know they are curious enough about weather that they can easily speak, write, draw, move, and sing about the things they experience—even about weather that is not typical here."

The music teacher listened intently before responding to his colleague, "I have an idea. Let's sit down after school and talk about some ways to infuse arts instruction into the theme of weather variations. I like the idea of storms and have great songs, movement ideas, visual art, creative drama, Readers' Theatre, chants, and poetry we could use. If you show me your science and social studies curriculum and some children's literature, I think we might get an idea for a schoolwide theme and shared performance."

The classroom teacher thanked her friend and was touched by his constructive ideas and sensitivity to her classroom curriculum concerns. The two agreed to meet after school the next day. And so it all began . . .

These two teachers knew that district and school-site administration encouraged integrated instruction of all arts into other subject areas (and vice versa) and promoted the development of instructional ideas involving science and literacy (reading, writing, and oral language development). Additionally, the music teacher was aware that many of the National Standards in music specify various active music learning connections to other subject areas, including the arts. He reviewed the National Standards in music (MENC, 1994a) again and began to think about this new unit:

> National Standard #4: Composing and arranging music within specified guidelines.

> National Standard #6: Listening to, analyzing, and describing music.

> National Standard #8: Understanding relationships between music, the other arts, and disciplines outside the arts.

> National Standard #9: Understanding music in relation to history and culture.

Both teachers began to explore thematic curriculum ideas. As the music teacher reviewed national standards in dance, theater, and visual art, he began to explore possible ideas incorporating them into music class activities about the storm theme. Accordingly, the classroom teacher knew the science and social studies standards well and focused the discussion on those. At the same time, both teachers seemed aware of the limitations of time, resources, and expertise needed to make purposeful connections between the arts and other content areas. They agreed to map out a tangible plan of activities and curriculum as a direct model to other teachers concerned with integrated instruction. Their idea was to ensure that student learning in the music classroom would be tied to other arts and extended into learning activities in the general classroom, which would, in turn, set up learning for the upcoming music class. The following examples of four integrated teaching episodes and the resulting performance involved all students in grades K–4 and took place over a 3-week period.

TEACHING EPISODE 1: WHETHER THE WEATHER

This first teaching episode was designed to involve the students actively in learning about weather changes through their creative response to rhythmic speech, children's literature, oral language and vocabulary development, creative movement and drama, singing, and visual art.

Introduction

The music teacher shared the poem "Weather" (see Table A.1; Hopkins, 1994) to introduce students to changes in weather and how the two words *weather* and *whether* differed. After reading the poem aloud together, the music teacher divided the class into two groups. Each group then chanted an alternating line of the poem (A or B) in rhythm several times, after which the class made decisions about tempo, dynamics, flow, and other expressive qualities of the words. Classroom percussion instruments were added. This composition would be used in the schoolwide performance (see the shared performance section).

Read-Aloud

Class read-alouds of quality children's books can set the tone and imaginative context for a unit of study, introduce vocabulary, and allow for creative expression about the curriculum. Three books were chosen with the following qualities in mind: good character development, quality writing, interesting and artistic illustrations, and honest and accurate information tied to the standards and instruction at hand.

➤ *Come on, Rain* by Karen Hesse (1999). On a hot, muggy summer day, Tess begs the sky to rain. The storm finally comes, and the whole neighborhood celebrates with music and dancing.

➤ *Singing Down the Rain* by Joy Cowley (1997). This highly musical story focuses on a southern town suffering from a drought. Brianna decides to sing rain songs and believes, "If you sing, the rain will come down."

TABLE A.1. Weather Poem by Anonymous

Line	Text
A	Whether the weather be fine,
B	Or whether the weather be not,
A	Whether the weather be cold,
B	Or whether the weather be hot,
A	We'll weather the weather
B	Whatever the weather
A and B	Whether we like it or not.

Song Activity

Following the read-aloud, the music teacher introduced his students to the song "Big Old Storm A-Comin' " (see Table A.2) and added creative movement. Following the song, the music teacher asked his students, "What kind of weather is happening in this song?" He listed the students' descriptors and created a group movement for each weather event.

Extension Suggestions

The music teacher suggested that teachers ask students to "tell a partner about a storm you saw." The students then drew the storm they experienced or a storm they imagined and wrote a few sentences. This artwork was saved for a display at the upcoming performance.

Extension Activity

The music teacher invited classroom teachers to read aloud books focused on another weather event. This shared preparation allowed the whole school to focus on weather and allowed classroom teachers to maximize their instructional time by connecting science and language arts instruction with the arts. The music teacher pro-

TABLE A.2. Music Selections from *Making Music*

"Big Old Storm A-Comin' " song	K, p. 257, BB p. 47	CD 8-18
"Cloudburst" (Grofé) from *The Grand Canyon Suite* listening	K, p. 260, BB p. 48	CD 8-23
"Snowflakes" song and poem	G1, pp. 402, 403	CD 11-42
"Who Has Seen the Wind" song	G2, p. 312	CD 10-24
"Whirlwind" by Joe Green listening/xylophone	G3, pp. 144, 145	CD 4-26
"Windshield Wipers" rhythmic speech	G1, p. 11	CD 1-9
"The Storm" sound montage	G1, p. 55	CD 2-13
"I Love a Rainy Night" by Eddie Rabbitt (song and line dance)	G5, p. 338 Dance instructions G5, pp. 516	CD 13-22
"Let It Snow! Let It Snow! Let It Snow!" song	G4, pp. 410–411	CD 15-19

Making Music ©2002 (K–8 National Music Text) published by Pearson Education/Scott Foresman—Silver Burdett Music, Parsippany, New Jersey.

vided his colleagues with a number of book choices about the upcoming theme of wind and based on grade-level reading skills and class interest. These books included:

> *Hurricane* by David Wiesner (1990). The story is told from the viewpoint of two young brothers who endure a fierce hurricane only to resume their play and games among the fallen trees in their own backyard.

> *The Wind Blew* by Pat Hutchkins (1993). This book features delightful rhyming verse about the day the wind blew everything away, almost out to sea, but then changed its mind.

> *Eye of the Storm* by Stephen Kramer (1997). This book introduces students to storm chasers and provides a great deal of factual, scientific information about storms.

TEACHING EPISODE 2: WIND ALL AROUND ME

This second teaching episode features active, creative response within musical listening, singing, creative movement and drama, and oral language contexts. The focus of this episode includes guided activity in response to visual art about a weather component wind.

Introduction

The students were shown photos of whirlwinds or windy scenes. They were then asked, "What is a whirlwind? How does it move?" Students experimented with created movements in response to verbal prompts (e.g., whirlwinds spin and travel across the land as they grow in size and energy). Then, the teacher described the featured instrument in the upcoming listening sample (the concert xylophone) and compared a classroom xylophone to a symphonic xylophone and those from different cultures (e.g., West African, Latin American, Indonesian, etc.).

Musical Listening

The CD recording of percussionist Evelyn Glennie's rendition of "Whirlwind" (see Table A.2) was played. Afterward the teacher asked, "How did the music remind you of a whirlwind? What did the music do?" The teacher then listed the students' ideas about fast and slow tempos, dynamic changes, etc., and invited students to draw whirlwind patterns matched to the movement of the music.

Wind Paintings

Table A.3 contains a sample list of paintings shown in the book *How Artists See the Weather* (Carroll, 1996). This book provides inquiry-based activities designed to engage children in a discussion of each work of art and also provides extensive information about the artists and their technique. The music teacher asked about the Wyeth painting: "Close your eyes for a moment and imagine yourself inside this room. Does the wind feel cool and soothing on your face, or does it blow hot and dry? What does it sound like as it blows into the room? Pretend you are those billowing lace curtains and move as they do in this summer wind" (p. 13). The students were then invited to create movement and instrumental soundscapes in response to the painting.

Song/Movement Activity

After learning the song "Who Has Seen the Wind?" (see Table A.2), the teacher asked his students to create a dramatic song text play about the character of the wind and improvise their own wind movements during the CD recording's instrumental interludes. He prompted the children's movement response by asking, "What do you see and feel?" and listed their ideas on the board.

Extension Activity

The music teacher asked his students to ask their classroom teachers where the wind comes from. They then wrote journal entries about the wind for a display at the shared performance.

TABLE A.3. Fine Art Examples of Weather	
Wind	*Wind from the Sea* by Andrew Wyeth (b. 1917)
	A Gust of Wind at Ejiri by Katsushika Hokusai (1760–1849)
Rain	*Night of the Equinox* by Charles Burchfield (1893–1967)
	Landscape with Rain by Wassily Kandinsky (1866–1944)
Snow	*Boulevard de Clichy, Paris* by Paul Signac (1863–1935)
	Haystacks in the Snow by Claude Monet (1840–1926)
	The Snowstorm by Francisco José de Goya (1746–1828)
Note. Data from Carroll (1996).	

TEACHING EPISODE 3: IMAGINATIONS ARE POURING RAIN

This episode features a listening activity about the sounds of nature within compositions about rain. In addition to creative group responses to fine art and poetry about rain, students learn a song and patterned line dance and view a video.

Introduction

The teacher played the CD recording of "The Storm" (see Table A.2) and asked, "What is happening here?" As they listened to the recording, students viewed photographs of a storm and checked off descriptor words such as "clouds gathering," "thunder," "lightning," "downpour," "flash flood," and "raindrops." A music classroom storm sound montage was created using the following: improvised vocal wind sounds, wind chimes, cookie sheets "played" with upward and downward movements, and paper plates filled with unpopped popcorn and stapled together. This soundscape used written iconic notation prompts indicating dynamic and tempo changes.

Poem Chant

The students listened to the recorded rhythmic speech chant "Windshield Wipers" by Mary Ann Hoberman (see Table A.2) as they read the words from a wall chart. The students were asked about the differences between the first and second readings of the poem (difference in tempo—slow then fast) and created steady beat windshield wiper movements to accompany a rereading of the poem.

Musical Listening

The teacher showed examples of illustrations and photos of rainstorms to introduce a listening episode of "Cloudburst" from the Grand Canyon Suite by Ferde Grofé (see Table A.2). Students listed descriptive words about the storm portrayed through music (e.g., rising storm, dark clouds, flash floods, etc.).

Visual Art Guided Response

Returning to the book *How Artists See the Weather* (Carroll, 1996), students viewed the painting "Night of the Equinox" by Charles Burchfield and were asked to "trace your finger along the lines. Do you think this was a gentle rain, or does it hit the ground with great force? What would you do on a rainy night like this?" (p. 31).

Line Dance and Song

The students enjoyed learning a simple line dance to the CD recording of Eddie Rabbitt's "I Love a Rainy Night" (see Table A.2).

Extension Activity

Classroom teachers were encouraged to show a portion of the Disney movie *Fantasia* that portrays other storm scenes (Beethoven's Symphony #6—*Pastoral*, and Dukas's *The Sorcerer's Apprentice*). Classroom teachers choose from the following children's literature about rain and experimented with student response modes to these books (e.g., Readers' Theatre, Expressive Reading, recreated scenes, illustrations of the texts).

> ➤ *Flood* by Mary Calhoun (1997) recounts the devastating midwest floods of 1993. The story is somber, as are the paintings, but offers hope for rebuilding a community.

> ➤ *Water Dance* by Thomas Locker (1997) is a beautifully illustrated book that enhances the lyrical text (perfect for a choral reading) about rainstorms and the formation of bodies of water.

> ➤ *Storm on the Desert* by Carolyn Lesser (1997) is a poetic drama for older children of an impressive summer storm in the American Southwest desert. It is perfect for pairing with musical listening to Grofé's "Cloudburst" from the *Grand Canyon Suite*.

TEACHING EPISODE 4: IT'S SNOWING!

This final episode features creative movement to sound and selected poetry, creative response to fine art, songs and instrumental pieces, and general classroom extensions featuring student art projects and choral reading of American poetry.

Introduction

As the students listened to and read the text to the song "Snowflakes" (see Table A.2), they listed descriptive words about snowflakes (e.g., whirling, swirling, rushing, twirling) and created actions to use with the song. The teacher played the CD recording again as the students creatively moved and sang.

Visual Art Guided Response

Returning to the book *How Artists See the Weather* (Carroll, 1996), the students viewed the painting "Haystacks in the Snow" by Claude Monet and discussed the following: "Many artists use the color blue to paint snow. Why would they do such a thing, when everyone knows that snow is white?" (p. 25).

Song Activities

The students completed the prompt, "When it snows, I look forward to . . . " These phrases were compiled into a group poem titled "We Love the Snow." The students also learned the classic song "Let It Snow! Let It Snow! Let It Snow!" by Sammy Cahn and Jule Styne as recorded by Harry Connick, Jr. (see Table A.2).

EXTENSION ACTIVITIES

Classroom teachers read aloud the book *Snowballs* (Ehlert, 1995) and provided students with a choice of found materials (e.g., twigs, shells, leaves, bottlecaps, corn kernels, material scraps, twine) to create their own interesting versions of snow people. These student art pieces would be displayed at the performance sharing event.

THE SHARED PERFORMANCE

The school multipurpose room was the setting for an informal performance. Students wrote the following scripted narration and used it with PowerPoint-projected color images of fine art, photographs scanned from scientific weather books, and nature photography. These images served as a dramatic background for a CNN style of reporting weather events!

NARRATOR: I'm _____ reporting live from _____
Elementary School's Weather Center. Our top story tonight focuses on the storms brewing across the country and whether the weather is good.

PERFORMANCE: [Group chant (alternating A and B sections) of the poem "Weather."]

NARRATOR: This just in from _____ county weather watch. There's a big old storm a-comin', so better shut those windows tight!

PERFORMANCE: [Several classes performed the song and created dance to "Big Old Storm A-Comin.' "]

NARRATOR: (*reading weather information from the text of* Eye of the Storm *by Stephen Kramer* [1997]) "Storms are caused by certain kinds of weather patterns. The same patterns are found in the same areas year after year. For example, every spring, large areas of cool, dry air and warm, moist air collide over the central United States. If the winds are right, tornado-producing thunderstorms appear" (p. 17).

PERFORMANCE: [One class performed their soundscape composition directed by a student. As the windstorm slowly died down, the narrator continued.]

NARRATOR: Great News! Expect windy but calmer conditions later in the day.

PERFORMANCE: [Song and created movement: "Who Has Seen the Wind."]

NARRATOR: Meanwhile, on the other side of America, expect rain. We're not concerned about flash floods at this point, but you'll need your umbrellas!

PERFORMANCE: [Recorded sounds of a rainstorm: "The Storm." A second group of students performed rainstorm soundscape. At the end of the rainstorm, a slow-tempo steady beat began on hand drums of various sizes. Students playing guiros and sand blocks joined in on the steady beat of windshield wiper sounds.]

NARRATOR: Folks, let's go to a live shot on _____ Ave. downtown. Looks like that rush hour traffic is bumper to bumper with windshield wipers in full gear!

PERFORMANCE: [Several classes performed "Windshield Wipers," first at the slower, then faster tempo.]

NARRATOR: Lots of people have been cooped up during our recent storms. Tonight we're expecting light rain, and we here at the Weather Center know how we all love a rainy night.

PERFORMANCE: [Several classes performed the song and line dance to "I Love a Rainy Night."]

NARRATOR: This just in . . . It's not what we expected, but callers are reporting our first snowfall may be on the way. Let's go live to our weather observer in the mountains. Anthony, are you there?

ANTHONY: Yes, it's true. It's just too darn cold for rain. The snowflake crystals are swirling all around me. In fact, by golly . . . I think they're scampering, rushing, and twirling as I speak!

PERFORMANCE: [Several classes performed the song and created movement to "Snowflakes."]

NARRATOR: Even though we have been snowed in for days, leave it to the youngsters to create some very interesting snow people. Let's take a look at these little masterpieces.

PERFORMANCE: [The younger children held up their *Snowballs* art pieces during a walking art parade around the room as they marched to the beat of the song "Let It Snow! Let It Snow! Let It Snow!" sung by older children. Audience members were invited to join in the singing.]

NARRATOR: So now at the end of our report, there really will be weather, whether we like it or not!

PERFORMANCE: [Groups recited again the rhythmic chant, "Weather" (see Table A.1). THE END]

CONCLUSION

Integration does not have to diminish the effect of solid teaching in the arts. In fact, experiences in purposeful curriculum integration can serve to increase the power of our creative teaching, increase job satisfaction and interaction with our teaching peers, and increase direct student interest and active involvement in learning linked within the school environment (Jacobs, 1989). In order for these and other kinds of purposeful changes to occur, we need

time, structured curriculum planning and teaching collaborations between classroom and music/arts specialists, developmentally appropriate understanding and skills in arts curricula tied to other subject matter, open-mindedness toward problem-solving, long-range goals, professional development in integration, inclusion of parent, student, community input and resources, humor, teacher reflection, and ways to evaluate and access integrated teaching and learning (Snyder, 2001). However, we know changes in how we teach can indeed have their roots in one person's ideas, which then, through example begin to lead others. (McDonald & Fisher, 2002, pp. 18–19)

Finally, with the idea of improving and enhancing quality arts instruction for every child, we have nothing to lose as we include others in our collaborative teaching efforts.

REFERENCES

Calhoun, M. (1997). *Flood*. New York: Morrow Junior Books.

Carroll, C. (1996). *How artists see the weather*. New York: Abbeville.

Cowley, J. (1997). *Singing down the rain*. New York: HarperCollins.

Ehlert, L. (1995). *Snowballs*. New York: Voyager.

Hancock, M. (2000). *A celebration of literature and response: Children, books and teachers in the K–8 classrooms*. New York: Prentice Hall.

Hesse, K. (1999). *Come on, rain*. New York: Scholastic.

Hopkins, L. (1994). *Weather: Poems for all seasons*. New York: Harper Trophy.

Hutchkins, P. (1993). *The wind blew*. New York: Aladdin.

Jacobs, H. H. (1989). *Interdisciplinary curriculum: Design and implementation*. Alexandria, VA: Association for Supervision and Curriculum Development.

Kramer, S. (1997). *Eye of the storm*. New York: Putnam.

Lesser, C. (1997). *Storm on the desert*. San Diego: Harcourt Brace.

Locker, T. (1997). *Water dance*. San Diego: Harcourt Brace.

McDonald, N., & Fisher, D. (2002). *Developing arts-loving readers: Top 10 questions teachers are asking about integrated arts education*. Lanham, MD: Scarecrow.

Music Educators National Conference. (1994a). *Dance, music, theater, visual arts: What every young American should know and be able to do in the arts. National standards for arts education*. Reston, VA: Author.

Music Educators National Conference. (1994b). *The school music program: A new vision: The K–12 national standards, pre-K standards, and what they mean to music educators*. Reston, VA: Author.

Simon, S. (1992). *Storms*. New York: Mulberry.

Snyder, S. (2001). Connection, correlation, and integration. *Music Educators Journal, 87*(5), 32–39.

Wiesner, D. (1990). *Hurricane*. New York: Clarion.

MOVIN' ALONG

The Poetry of Transportation

Transportation is a popular theme in the primary grades. Teachers across the country focus on travel in the air, on land, or at sea during their kindergarten and first-grade social studies lessons. Students in grades 2 and 3 rarely receive deeper instruction about transportation. However, we know that these 7- to 9-year-olds remain very interested in how people move from place to place. Children love to write, draw, and create dramatic interpretations of their transportation experiences. For example, Justin visited his grandmother and desperately wanted to tell the class about the various forms of transportation he used to get there, including a commuter train. He wrote in his journal, "I sat at the window and I could see everything go by. The train went through big tunnels, drove over mountains, and went very fast right by the ocean. When we were next to the freeway, we were going faster than the trucks. We stopped at seven towns before I got to my grandmother's house. I learned the name of all the towns."

Justin's third-grade teacher, Ms. Noriega, realized that her students rarely had the opportunity to express their excitement and wonderings about travel. Justin's teacher shared his journal with her colleagues during lunch. They all agreed that Justin's writing was unusually rich and hypothesized that this was probably due to his interest in the topic. One of the teachers at this lunch suggested that Justin's teacher visit the school library and borrow the book *Train Song* (Siebert, 1990) to give to him that afternoon. After seeing his excitement after reading a book related to his travel experiences, Justin's teacher decided to create an integrated thematic unit of study about trains. She decided to use the genre of poetry so that she could meet a literacy standard along the way.

BACKGROUND

Our purpose here is to provide teachers with ideas for reteaching primary-grade content in meaningful ways to older students, remembering that older students remain interested in some topics but at a much deeper level. As Justin taught us, he understood the technical language of transportation, but was still interested in learning and talking more about this topic. Justin's teacher could have given him an encyclopedia and asked him to look up information about trains. However, Ms. Noriega was wise enough to know that Justin and the other students in her class needed more than that. Rather than rely on one source of information, Ms. Noriega wanted to integrate her curriculum. Curriculum integration allowed her to use her time well—meeting social studies, language arts, and visual and performing arts standards at the same time. Curriculum integration also allowed her students to understand the connections between traditionally separate areas of understanding and learning (Jacobs, 1989, 1997). While she knew that trains were not on the state standardized test, she knew that the vocabulary they would learn, the language they would be exposed to, and the thinking they would have to do would be a great benefit come test time.

Ms. Noriega elected to begin her unit with poetry. She knew that, in primary grades, poetry is taught as a way to address phonemic awareness, not as a genre. However, poetry can be thought of as highly expressive language with well-chosen and strategic words depicting deeper meanings of sensory experiences (McDonald & Fisher, 1999; Rosenblatt, 1978). As students become aware of the sensory meanings of words, teachers can guide them into direct experiences involving movement, word play, singing, dramatic interpretation, visual arts, and even creative performances (Stephens, 1994; Wiggins, 2001).

CURRICULUM UNIT MODEL: "ALL ABOUT TRAINS"

Ms. Noriega began her discussion about trains by asking her students the following questions as she listed their responses on a chart:

Where can we see trains? What kinds of trains pass through our town?
Where are those trains going? What are they carrying?
What are some things we see, hear, and feel as we watch trains go by?
What are some things we see, hear, and feel when we go on a train ride?

The children became very engaged in sharing what they already knew about trains. As they shared their responses, the teacher would prompt more discussion by asking:

What kinds of things might be inside the train's cargo bins?
When does the engineer sound the train horn? Why?
How is the train powered?
What makes its wheels turn?
Do you start a train like you start a car, with a key?

These kinds of probes resulted in even more student participation and descriptive phrases to add to the class "All about Trains" chart.

After this discussion, Ms. Noriega asked the students to illustrate various descriptive phrases listed on the chart. For instance, Pilar chose to illustrate the phrases "giant wheels on rails of steel" and "cargo bins full of grain." The teacher encouraged class members each to illustrate different chart ideas so that their illustrations could reflect the content of the "All about Trains" class chart. The students' individual phrases and illustrations were compiled into a class book, which was bound and added to the class library.

Following this, Ms. Noriega read aloud *Train Song* by Diane Siebert (1981). This book contains beautiful illustrations within highly evocative, poetic text about the sights, sounds, and rhythmic energy of trains and train travel. The children then read aloud the book's text as a Readers' Theatre, first all together and then in small groups with individuals assigned certain pages. The children were encouraged to find ways to make the poetry come alive as the teacher modeled the following text with dramatic expression and creative movement:

steel wheels rolling
on steel trails
rumbling
grumbling
on steel rails

She read aloud other rhythmical sections of the text and asked the students to echo her voice model of these sections in rhythm. She then asked the children for ideas for simple movements to accompany that text. The students particularly enjoyed choral speaking and creatively moving to the following section of the text:

great trains
freight trains
talk about your late trains
the 509
right on time
straight through to L.A.
whistle blows
there she goes
slicing through the day

Ms. Noriega pointed out that train sounds can also be very entertaining. She asked her students to listen to the delightful King's Singers' recording of the song "I'm a Train" (see resource list). The students were asked how they thought the singers created realistic sounds and motions of a train with their voices. Several of the students were able to recreate some of the amusing vocal sounds used to capture the sound of the train's wheels, whistle, and changing speed. This recording was so popular with the students that they requested to hear it time and time again.

By now the students had thought about, discussed, read aloud, moved to, visualized, and illustrated concepts about trains. The teacher then led the children in a guided musical listening experience using the orchestral composition *Pacific 231*, by the composer Honneger (see resource list). This 20th-century piece is a musical representation of the sounds and rhythms of a modern locomotive's journey over the rails. To guide the students through the action or sections of this 6-minute recording, the teacher created six "guidepost signs" for the children to read aloud before listening to the piece:

1. The engine is at a standstill gathering steam.

2. The big wheels begin to turn slowly as the locomotive gets underway.

3. The locomotive begins to move more quickly, gathering speed as it goes.

4. The sleek silver train rushes through the dark night.

5. The great engine slows down.

6. The great steel wheels finally grind to a stop.

As the recording of *Pacific 231* is played, the teacher held up the "guidepost" of the appropriate section of the piece. The students were asked to read the sign silently as the music is playing. They then closed their eyes to listen, visualize, and write down their ideas about how the train might look and sound during this section of the music. Between guidepost four and five is a longer listening section during which the students were asked to illustrate their visualization of the train as it "rushed through the night." Even though this fourth guidepost section is the longest of the entire piece, the students were focused throughout the musical listening lesson because of the instruction that accompanied it.

After hearing the entire piece, the children shared what they imagined, wrote, or illustrated during each "guidepost" section. Maria wrote, "*Pacific 231* was a powerful train. It took a lot of time for it to get going, but then I could hear how fast it could go. When it slowed down, I pretended I was at the train station waiting for my uncle to get off the train. Then I ran to meet him!" Kyle wrote, "*Pacific 231* had to go up hills, through lots of tunnels and up and down mountains. Its horn blasted a lot through the night. People in towns were really mad when the train woke them up. When it finally came to a stop, all the engineers needed to take a nap before their next trip."

Ms. Noriega knew that many students in her class had learned the famous song "I've Been Working on the Railroad" in their music classes. With guidance from the music teacher, she knew that the children had already created movements and classroom instrument accompaniments for this song. The students incorporated some of the vocables from the King's Singers' recording (e.g., chuck-a, chuck-a, ssshhh) into their singing of "I've Been Working on the Railroad." Ms. Noriega quickly realized she had unleashed a significant amount of creativity!

At this point student interest in trains had grown considerably. Ania, an avid Harry Potter reader, raised her hand during class one day and excitedly shared that even Harry rides a train—the Hogwarts Express—to wizard school! Guiding the conversation back to the history of trains and railroads, Ms. Noriega introduced a wonderful book about the history of trains and railroads, *Steam, Smoke and Steel: Back in Time with Trains* by Patrick O'Brien (2000). The text is presented through the voice of a young boy who decides to become a railroad engineer just as the past seven generations of his family had done. The boy tells the story, aided by accurate historical photographs and interesting railroad lore, of each of his relatives and the trains they loved and rode. The students were fascinated with the photos of historic trains. Jamika commented, "I've seen a steam engine like that at the railroad museum! That other one looks like the train at Disneyland."

Not only were the students interested in modern trains and train travel, they began asking questions about all kinds of trains, past and present. Once the children were familiar with the look of old trains, the teacher drew their attention to a map of the United States. As she began to introduce the traditional American folk song "Wabash Cannon Ball" (see resource list), she pointed out that there are a lot of tall tales about famous trains and that those tall tales have been added to as time goes on. The tale of the Wabash Cannon Ball has evolved over the years to include ideas about where this fantasy train might go, mysterious names of the IJA&SM

Railroad on which it ran (Ireland, Jerusalem, Australian, and Southern Michigan Railroad) and that it was once owned by the younger brother of Paul Bunyan, Cal Bunyan. The Wabash Cannon Ball was once said to have 700 cars and a ticket collector who had to ride a motorcycle over the top of the train to collect all the passenger tickets. The mysterious train was known to travel so fast that it was seen arriving at its destination an hour before it even left the station.

The students began spontaneously to add to the "Wabash Cannon Ball" tall tale with ideas of their own. Kim giggled, "The Wabash Cannon Ball was so long that the engine would be in California when its caboose was in Texas!" Ramona added, "The Wabash Cannon Ball gave off so much steam, it caused a flood in Kansas." The teacher asked the children to write down their tall tale ideas to create a "tall tale" narration to accompany a performance of the song they were about to learn.

As children pointed to their music texts, they then read aloud the verses and refrain of the "Wabash Cannon Ball" song. The students pointed to the words as they read aloud. After reading aloud rhythmically, the children listened to the CD recording of the song as they continued to point to the song text and mouthed the words. Quickly, the children began to sing along on the refrain:

Just listen to the jingle, the rumble, and the roar
Of the mighty locomotive as she steams along the shore,
Hear the thunder of the engine, hear the lonesome whistle call,
It's the Western combination called the *Wabash Cannon Ball*.

The teacher then asked the students to find all the names of cities and other places mentioned in the song. Eagerly, the children offered, "Pacific, Atlantic, Southland, Labrador, Chicago, Saint Louis, Rock Island, and Santa Fe" and found their locations on the map in order to trace the route of this mysterious, mythical train. Jason asked, "Wow! How could one train go all those places?" The class laughed and reminded him that it was a tall-tale train!

THE TRANSPORTATION PERFORMANCE

The class became excited about sharing their creative ideas about trains with other classes. Given that first graders at her school all studied transportation, Ms. Noriega asked her colleagues if they would like to attend a special transportation performance staged by her third-grade class. In addition to the poem "Trains and Trucks and Planes" (Table B.1), the class decided to share the following activities with the younger students:

TABLE B.1. "Trains and Trucks and Planes" by Nan McDonald

Over rails and roads and sky
There's adventure for a watchful eye
When I'm alone and bored or blue
I plan a trip for me and you . . .

A trip by rail would be just fine
Big engine pulling train cars in line
Our window seats provide a view
Of endless chances to see something new

Big rig gleaming over wheels so high
Horn blasting "hello" to cars passing by
A truck trip would be so great
But big deliveries just can't be late!

We could soar above cities, hills, and all below
In our plane traveling isn't as slow
Mountains, deserts, islands, and sea
The whole world waits for you and me.

➤ A sing-along performance of "I've Been Working on the Railroad"

➤ A read-aloud of the class book of poems and illustrations

➤ A Readers' Theatre performance of *Train Song*

➤ A lip-sync of "I'm a Train"

➤ Narration of interesting facts from history books and internet searches

➤ Singing and tall tales of the "Wabash Cannon Ball"

➤ An improvised creative movement and instrument sound activity for the younger students in which they become trains and travel around the room

➤ A sentence about trains dictated by first graders to a third-grade buddy, illustrated, and bound into a first-grade class library book

CONCLUSION

We would like to encourage you to enjoy the creative processes that naturally evolve out of this kind of innovative, experience-based teaching. Whatever the outcome of the final production, you will have created expressive avenues of discovery about the poetry through multiple learning approaches in several curriculum areas. Simply put, you have taught in a manner that may reach more kids in more ways than simply blandly reading a social studies book and assigning new vocabulary. Instead, you have set the scene for the children to make meaning about their experiences and how those experiences are reflected in books all around them. As Berghoff (2001) notes, "Our curricula also need to take students to the aesthetic end of the continuum as often as possible because 'lived' experiences are integrative experiences. As learners, we come to know more fully when our emotions and imaginations are stimulated" (p. 37).

REFERENCES

Berghoff, B. (2001). Going beyond words. *Primary Voices K–6, 9*(4), 34–37.

Jacobs, H. H. (1989). *Interdisciplinary curriculum: Design and implementation.* Alexandria, VA: Association for Supervision and Curriculum Development.

Jacobs, H. H. (1997). *Mapping the big picture: Integrating curriculum and assessment K-12.* Alexandria, VA: Association for Supervision and Curriculum Development.

McDonald, N., & Fisher, D. (1999). Living haiku: Scenes of sound in motion. In S. Totten, C. Johnson, L. R. Morrow, & T. Sills-Briegel (Eds.), *Practicing what we preach: Preparing middle level educators* (pp. 273–275). New York: Falmer.

O'Brien, P. (2000). *Steam, smoke, and steel: Back in time with trains.* Watertown, MA: Chasrlesbridge.

Rosenblatt, L. M. (1978). *The reader, the text, the poem: The transactional theory of the literary work.* Carbondale, IL: Southern Illinois University Press.

Siebert, D. (1990). *Train song.* New York: Crowell.

Stephens, D. (1994). Learning what art means. *Language Arts, 71,* 34–37.

Wiggins, R. A. (2001). Interdisciplinary curriculum: Music educator concerns. *Music Educators Journal, 87*(5), 40–44.

ANNOTATED SOURCE LIST

Books

Aylesworth, Jon. (1991). *Country crossing.* New York: Atheneum.

Sights and sounds of a powerful freight train as it passes a country railroad crossing on a summer night. The whole scene is witnessed lovingly by an old man and a little boy who wait patiently in their car at the railroad crossing. Rich in soundscapes and vocabulary. Excellent for a study of dynamics, louds and softs in music and movement, visual art, and speech/drama.

Cooney, Barbara. (1982). *Miss Rumphius.* New York: Viking.

A former town librarian tells her story of the adventurous travel excitement of her youth. Text and charming illustrations can be used for discussion and writing extensions about places the students would like to go and people they know who have traveled to many interesting places.

Fraser, Mary Ann. (1993). *Ten mile day and the building of the transcontinental railroad.* New York: Holt.

A well-researched account for third- to sixth-grade readers of the building of the Transcontinental Railroad's last 10 miles in the spring of 1869. Excellent information on the geography, biography, events, historical viewpoints including those of Chinese laborers, Native Americans, and business management, and journalistic accounts of the exciting meeting of the rails.

Hartry, Nancy. (1997). *Hold on, McGinty!* New York: Doubleday.

The cross-Canada adventure of an old fisherman who must relocate (with his boat!) from his beloved home on Newfoundland's Atlantic coast westward to his daughter's home on Vancouver Island. To get there, McGinty rides inside his boat on a freight train.

Heap, Christine. (1998). *Big book of trains.* New York: DK Publishing.

The book has a gigantic format—more than 50 trains including steam engines, diesel to modern electric trains, and bullet trains around the world. Focus is on both human drivers and operators as well as computer technologies. Shows the evolution of trains and rail transport.

Morris, Ann. (1990). *On the go.* New York: Lothrop, Lee, & Shepard.

Beautiful photographs feature many kinds of transportation around the world.

Poetry

Livingston, Myra Conn (Ed.). (1993). *Roll along: Poems on wheels.* New York: Margaret McElderry.

This anthology includes 50 poems about transportation—bikes, skateboards, cars, busses, trucks, jeeps, subways, wagons, motorcycles, etc., as well as travel modes kids can only dream about! Many unique sounds, words, and rhythms as well as created words to imitate or capture the sights and sounds of the transport. Great resource!

Peet, Bill. (1971). *The caboose who got loose.* New York: Houghton Mifflin.

Melodic prose. The caboose of a train hates always being last! An accident happens and she gets perched between two evergreen trees.

Prelutsky, Jack (1983). *The Random House book of poetry for children.* New York: Random House.

Contains many poems about transportation themes. Look for "Sing a Song of Subways" by Eve Merriam and "Things to Do If You Are a Subway" by Bobbi Katz.

Siebert, Diane. (1981). *Train song.* New York: HarperCollins.

Excellent poetic text and beautiful illustrations rich in sound descriptions and sensory stimuli. Excellent for reading and read-alouds. Great potential for movement, dramatization, and prompts for visual art and creative writing.

Suen, Anastasia. (1998). *Window music.* New York: Viking.

"Window Music" is railroad slang for the passing scenery. The book is full of simple rhyme and beautiful, rich earth-toned illustrations. The train makes "music" through the rhyme and rhythm of the text. Conveys a girl's train ride home from her grandparents' house. Travels through all types of terrain to the final destination of a city train depot.

Music

The following song and poetry material is from "The Music Connection," K–8 National Music Series by Scott Foresman/Silver Burdett and Ginn Music (©1995, 2000) Parsippany, New Jersey. Songs may be used at any appropriate grade level determined by text difficulty and musical content. CDs may be a great help. Poetry selections are printed in the Teacher and Student texts, but are not recorded on CDs. Also, song texts may also be used as poetry.

Title	Grade/p.	Grade/CD #
"Engine, Engine" (chant)	K, p. 305	
"Get on Board"	2, p. 58	2/2-25
"Going Places" (poem)	K, p. 89	
"How Long the Train Been Gone?"	2, p. 263	2/8-11
"I've Been Working on the Railroad"	4, p. 138	6/2
"Little Red Caboose"	K, p. 200	K/5-5
"Long Trip" (poem)	5, p. 70	
"Long Way Home"	1, p. 149	1/4-4
"Morningtown Ride"	K, p. 228	K/5-38
"Nine Hundred Miles"	5, p. 202	5/9-1
"Paige's Train"	K, p. 312	K/7-31
"Railroad Cars Are Coming" (poem)	4, p. 141	
"The Rock Island Line"	4, p. 140	4/6-3
"Same Train"	2, p. 122	2/4-14
"Travel Plans" (poem)	K, p. 163	
"Wabash Cannon Ball"	5, p. 208	5/9-9
"When the Train Comes Along"	1, p. 148	1/4-3

Musical Listening Examples for Transportation Themes

All examples are found within *The Music Connection* (K–8 National Text Series) by Scott Foresman/Silver Burdett Ginn © 1995, 2000.

Title	Grade/p.	CD #
"Blue Town, New York Montage" from *Moscow on the Hudson* by McHugh	4, p. 41	2-14
"I'm a Train" by the King's Singers	4, p. 141	6-4
"Little Red Caboose" by Sweet Honey in the Rock	K, p. 200	5-6
"The Little Train of the Caipira" from *Bachianas Brasileiras, No. 2* by Villa-Lobos	2, p. 123	4-15
Pacific 231 (modern train) by Honegger	4, p. 142	6-5
"There's a Morning Train A-Comin' " by Eddleman	1, p. 66	2-11

Video Sources

Lots & Lots of Trains: Vol. 1 (1999). ASIN: 1581681259

This video contains some of the most exciting trains you'll ever see! In this volume, you'll see lots of trains winding through mountains, climbing steep grades, gliding over tracks, hauling, pulling, loading, and much more!

Kids Love Trains (1994). ASIN: 6303257577

This train video shows many types of trains. My children love the songs and music in this video. You'll enjoy watching this one with your child.

Thematic/Integrated Resources for Teachers

Burnham, J. (1991). *Theme book: Transportation—ideas and activities across the curriculum.* Palos Verdes Estates, CA: Frank Schaffer Publications.

Hierstein, J. (1995). *Art activities from award-winning picture books.* Carthage, IL: Teaching and Learning Company.

Levene, D. (1993). *Music through children's literature: Themes and variations.* Englewood, CO: Teacher Ideas Press.

McCarthy, T. (1992). *Literature-based geography activities.* New York: Scholastic.

Ritter, D. (1991). *Literature-based art activities: Creative art projects inspired by 45 popular children's books: Pre-K–3.* Cypress, CA: Creative Teaching Press.

Tarlow, E. (1998). *Teaching story elements with favorite books: Creative and engaging activities to explore character, plot, setting, and theme: Grades 1–3.* New York: Scholastic.

EXPRESSIVE LITERACY WITHIN MUSICAL LISTENING
The Moldau, a Symphonic Poem by Smetana

Within our pre-service courses for liberal studies and music education majors, "Music Literature for Children," future teachers are encouraged to infuse literacy activities into all music and integrated arts experiences. During participatory models of elementary music lessons, students are consistently encouraged to read aloud and evocatively respond to song and listening activities through movement, visual art, drama, and creative writing (Cox, 1998; Greene, 1997). Curricular integration of this sort is not merely an overused educational buzzword, but rather a purposeful set of activities designed to increase the child's aesthetic learning through active involvement in expressive oral language (Jacobs, 1989, 1997; Landis & Carder, 1972; Lapp & Flood 1992; McDonald & Fisher, 1999; Rosenblatt, 1978; Vygotsky, 1962; Walter, 1959).

Song texts, for example, are poetry embedded within melodic and rhythmic settings. Their poetic contexts may include rich historical and cultural frameworks or dramatic settings of potential interest to young children, if taught actively and expressively (Cohn, 1993; Levene, 1993; Tarlow, 1998). A purposeful and well-prepared musical learning activity in which song texts are read aloud could be considered an active use of expressive literacy. Integrated activities may also contain added curricular bonuses through their natural connections to social studies, math, and science contexts—connections so needed by classroom teachers who may have limited background but great interest in the teaching of the arts (Barry, 1998).

NEW TERRITORY FOR ORAL LANGUAGE DEVELOPMENT: SYMPHONIC POEMS

Potential curriculum material for expressive literacy activities may also be found within perceived "forbidden" musical territory to the nonspecialist—that of the great symphonic literature of the late 19th century. Many orchestral masterpieces of this Romantic period in Western classical music are programmed compositions, *symphonic poems,* in which major sections of the music are thematically tied to the composer's intended "plot," or sequence of musical metaphor. Composer Franz Liszt, a prolific writer of this genre, composed 13 symphonic poems between 1848 and 1882. Liszt's format included relatively short pieces, which were not partitioned into separate movements, but rather in

a continuous form with various sections more or less contrasting in character and tempo, and a few themes which are developed, repeated, varied, or transformed in accordance with the particular design of each work. *Poem* in the designation may refer simply to the root meaning of the word—something "made," invented—or perhaps to the poetic content in the sense of the program of each work; for the content and form in every instance are suggested by some picture, statue, drama, poem, scene, personality, thought, impression, or other object not identifiable from the music alone; it is, however, identified by the composer's title and usually also by a prefatory note. (Grout, 1973, p. 586)

The great Czech composer Bedrich Smetana (1824–1884) wrote a piece entitled *Ma Vlast* (*My Fatherland*), a nationalistic musical composition about his homeland. As in much Romantic literature, art, and poetry of this period of European history, musical subjects interpreted intense patriotism, aesthetic responses to naturalistic settings, romantic longings, and idolized or heroic settings. Within *Ma Vlast* is an 11-minute symphonic poem, *The Moldau,* named after the great Czech river. The Moldau flows from its origins in the Alps through the countryside to the capital city of Prague and eventually to the sea. The music captures the imaginary experience of floating on the river and experiencing the sights, sounds, and feelings of its changing landscapes and forms.

Smetana wrote references to the images he wished to illuminate through his music in *The Moldau.* It is from the composer's original descriptive program notes that I constructed the following expressive literacy/musical listening and visual art activity for third- to eighth-grade students.

STRATEGIES AND ACTIVITIES FOR LISTENING TO *THE MOLDAU*

Preset/Expressive Speech

Before playing the musical recording of *The Moldau,* ask the children to read each card (see "Symphonic Poem Cards" below) expressively, out loud in unison, everyone staying together as in a dramatic choral reading. Insist that students read as "actors attempting to set the scene" for a musical journey. Students are to create beauty with their words—words that paint pictures during the music.

Students are asked to read the title and composer's name (card #1) and are told a little about Smetana's desire to "capture the sights and sounds and people of his beloved homeland." It is important that no visuals are shown other than the following text cards. Read them aloud without the music.

Each line may be written on a large poster or overhead and recited slowly in the order indicated below.

Symphonic Poem Cards

1. *The Moldau,* a symphonic poem by Smetana
2. Deep in the mountain forest . . . the little stream comes to life . . .
3. bubbling, churning . . .
4. swirling, splashing over rocks and boulders . . .
5. cascading over waterfalls . . .
6. Through the woods . . . the sounds of hunters on horseback . . .
7. Around the bend . . . a village wedding and its colorful peasant dancers
8. Moonlight—silver swirls . . . . Deep purple flowing water.. .
9. Building, churning into three giant waterfalls . . .
10. Past the great castle of Prague . . .
11. The Final Journey . . .
12. The great River Moldau flows boldly to the sea.
13. The end

Listening Activity/Visual Art with Text Cues to the Music

Rearrange the posters or overheads in their original text order. Tell students to get their drawing paper and crayons or pastels. There will be no talking in order to maintain focus and prepare for guided listening. Ask the students to write the name of the composition and the composer on the top of their art paper. Tell the students:

> "We are ready to listen, but we are about to listen with our ears and eyes! Smetana described his countryside through his music. We have his words about the journey of the Moldau and his ideas through his music. As the music plays, I would like you to illustrate how you see the music. You may sketch the entire piece or just a particular scene that you like. I will hold up the card of the section of the music we are 'in' as it is playing. You need to look up from your artwork whenever you think we may be in a new idea in the music. I will help you by softly snapping my fingers and holding up the new card. Okay, let's announce our piece [together, out loud]: 'The Moldau: A Symphonic Poem by Smetana.' "

The recording is played as the students illustrate and the teacher holds up appropriate card sections. It is imperative that the teacher prepare this lesson by listening to *The Moldau* several times in order to distinguish "text" sections in the music. This is easily done. If not, many children will be able to tell you quietly when they hear the next section. Remember not to talk (students or teacher) during the recording.

I like to hang the posters in reading sequence on a clothesline (with clothespins) so that the readers can see where they are in the thematic material and what is about to happen in the music. I can simply stand behind the cards and physically indicate where we are in the musical sequence.

LESSON EXTENSIONS

After the recording is played, ask the students to be silent as they hold up their artwork. Tell the students to look around the room at all the interpretations of Smetena's music. Admire as many student art pieces as possible and display them on a created composer's bulletin board (complete with fine art of the period) or within students' illustrated journals (portfolios) full of their responses to other musical compositions, poetry, or fine art from many cultural styles, origins, genres, and time periods.

I have asked upper elementary students to design a large paper mural depicting oversized scenes of *The Moldau*'s themes. As the recording is played, the students slowly unroll the mural and then physically dramatize a small, silent movement scene in front of the background as the music continues playing. *The Moldau*'s scene of "colorful peasant dancers" lends itself particularly well to students' creative movement and folk dance interpretations as the music is a Czech folk dance melody.

Older children may enjoy the experience of teaching the *Moldau* activity to a younger group of children at their school. Allow these students to research all they can about Smetana, the Czech Republic, the Moldau, Prague, Romantic period visual art, etc., and bring those found resources into their "lessons" for other students.

Use the curricular theme of water cycles to explore the great rivers of the United States and other countries: Amazon, Mississippi, Nile, Yellow River, Danube, Columbia, Colorado, Seine, Ganges, etc. Find indigenous music, literature, and visual art to surround these themes and resulting activities for extensions to social studies, reading, poetry, science, and math.

COMMENTARY

During our university lesson debriefing, one future elementary teacher commented:

> "This was an incredibly therapeutic lesson for me! I feel calm and focused and, for the first time, I was able to listen to a classical piece and not be overwhelmed by it. I usually get lost and frustrated within that wall of musical sound! I feel I could definitely use this idea and could enjoy teaching great music in this way. Thanks! We need more connections like this!"

In a similar way, a fourth-grader exclaimed:

> "Can we hear that again? Let's close our eyes and then see if we know where we are in the music and then open them, look at the cards, and check. I'm going to tell my grandma to get me that Moldau thing for me for Christmas!"

Traditional musical listening activities are powerful and evocative in their own right—however, musical listening combined with lessons utilizing oral language development may serve to enhance students' ability to focus and understand both the music and the written thematic material. If students feel a part of the musical composition—that is, intimately involved in the self-constructed meanings of the sound experience—they may be empowered to experience a rarity in many classroom settings, immersion in beauty, the aesthetic foundation of all art.

REFERENCES

Barry, N. (1998). Arts integration in the elementary classroom: Conference development and evaluation. *Update: Applications of Research in Music Education,* *17*(1), 3–8.

Cohn, A. (Ed.). (1993). *From sea to shining sea: A treasury of American folklore and folk songs.* New York: Scholastic.

Cox, C. (1998). *Children's stance towards literature: A longitudinal study, K–5.* Paper presented at the meeting of the 1998 American Educational Research Association, San Diego, CA.

Greene, M. (1997, January). Metaphors and multiples: Representation, the arts, and history. *Phi Delta Kappan,* pp. 387–394.

Grout, D. (1973). *A history of music.* New York: Norton.

Jacobs, H. H. (1989). *Interdisciplinary curriculum: Design and implementation.* Alexandria, VA: Association for Supervision and Curriculum Development.

Jacobs, H. H. (1997). *Mapping the big picture: Integrating curriculum and assessment K–12.* Alexandria, VA: Association for Supervision and Curriculum Development.

Landis, B., & Carder, P. (1972). *The eclectic curriculum in American music education: Contributions of Dalcroze, Kodaly, and Orff.* Washington, DC: Music Education National Conference.

Lapp, D., & Flood, J. (1992). *Teaching reading to every child* (3rd ed.). New York: Macmillan/McGraw-Hill.

Levene, D. (1993). *Music through children's literature: Themes and variations.* Englewood, CO: Teacher Ideas Press.

McDonald, N. & Fisher, D. (1999) Bug suites: An uncommonly integrated performance unit for fourth through eighth graders based on *Joyful Noise, Poems for Two Voices. Telling Stories: Theory, Practice, Interviews, and Reviews, 3*(2), 17–25.

Rosenblatt, L. (1978). *The reader, the text, the poem: The transactional theory of the literary work.* Carbondale, IL: Southern Illinois University Press.

Tarlow, E. (1998). *Teaching story elements with favorite books: Creative and engaging activities to explore character plot, setting, and theme: Grades 1–3.* New York: Scholastic.

Vygotsky, L. S. (1962). *Thought and language* (E. Hanfmann & G. Vakar, Eds. and Trans.). Cambridge, MA: MIT Press.

Walter, A. (1959). Carl Orff's music for children. *The Instrumentalist, 13,* 38–39.

HAIKU

Active Learning with and through the Arts

Poetry and the various forms of poems are often not identified by students as a favorite genre. There may be many reasons for this, but certainly one possibility is the way in which poetry is traditionally taught. Unfortunately, haiku is one of the poetic forms that is most vulnerable to rote memorization and not active engagement. Many teachers may read aloud various haiku in an expressive way; others ask the same of their students. The syllabic construction of the three lines of haiku usually winds its way into the discussion. In other classrooms, students may then write their own haiku. Still, even with the best of intentions, we know that our students' understanding of haiku may be limited and less than memorable, to say the least. The question becomes "What can we do to make haiku come alive for our students?"

The arts (music, dance, theater, visual arts) can provide powerful avenues for students to learn actively about haiku (McDonald & Fisher, 2002). When students are asked to read aloud expressively, illustrate, dramatize, and creatively move to poetic text, their learning is enhanced through personal interactions and total body involvement with the text meanings at hand (Cox, 1998; Cox & Many, 1992; Hancock, 2000; Jacobs, 1989, 1997; Lapp & Flood, 1992; McDonald & Fisher, 1999, 2002; Rosenblatt, 1978, 1995; Vygotsky, 1978). Simply put, students need to be

From *The California Reader,* 38(1), 18–23. Copyright 2004. Adapted by permission of The California Reading Association.

provided with opportunities actively to "do" and creatively respond to haiku in order to understand its meaning.

The remainder of this appendix will provide a three-stage curriculum model focused on haiku. Suggested lesson activities are designed for use in fourth-through eighth-grade classrooms and may be taught within three or more consecutive lessons. Connections to children's literature about haiku poets and poetry are included. Opportunities for small group/cooperative learning projects and shared performances are offered as well as resources and suggestions for further activities.

BACKGROUND ON HAIKU

Japanese haiku offers space for the reader's own thoughts, interpretations, and designs. Within the traditional form's three nonrhyming lines of text (and 17 syllables), one can sense a season or setting—a moment in which delicate outlines of action and reflection are offered to the reader. Typically, the action within a haiku seems to be unending or unresolved, leaving the reader wondering about an outcome.

EPISODE 1: SETTING THE SCENE: HAIKU IN MOTION

Play a CD recording of traditional music of Japan. Slow-tempo music of the koto (harp-like stringed instrument) and the shakuhachi (Japanese wooden flute) creates the best musical background for focus, mood, and movement.

Students silently mirror the very smooth and connected model movements of the teacher. Use very slow arm movements (as if moving through thick mud) for the students to mirror. Then ask the students to find a partner and decide who will lead first. Encourage students to mirror the leader exactly, even if the leader takes the movement to floor level or travels across the room. The music continues. Stress that the movement be connected and slow, done silently, as if underwater. During their movements, give your class quiet cues (e.g., "Now move in a low space," "Move with your partner across the room," "Change to the other person as leader now").

As the music continues, show pictures of classic Japanese watercolor paintings, watercolors with Japanese writing on them (poetry), traditional flower arrangements, Zen gardens, etc. Discuss the simplicity and beauty of the designs. Explain to your students that Japanese poets were often also artists and musicians.

Keep the music playing. Next, model a selected traditional haiku of a great master poet, Issa, from the book *Cool Melons—Turn to Frogs!: The Life and Poems of Issa* by Matthew Gollub (Lee & Low, 1998). One poem you could use is:

Asleep on the ocean—
A folding fan
shades me from the moon.
                    —Issa

The teacher models a selected haiku by Issa in three distinct ways:

1. *Speaking only.* Use highly expressive/dramatic speech that varies the tempo (speed and dynamics, softs and louds) according to the feeling and meaning of the haiku. Invite students to echo each line in the style you model.

2. *Dramatic speech with movement.* Repeat the haiku, but this time add simple movements to the mood of the expressive speech. For instance, "asleep" might be a nodded head movement rested on its side within opened cupped hands. "A folding fan" might be a fan shape created with both hands in an opening movement above the head and eyes. "Moon" might be a change in movement to a whole body movement creating a large round shape. Invite the students to try the movement sequence (line by line) with you, using expressive speech as they do so.

3. *Movement only.* Think the words, actually mouthing them if necessary, while performing the haiku movements without sound. Then, invite the students to try the movement sequence with you.

Now create small cooperative groups of five to seven students. Each group should be assigned a different Issa poem from the Gollub book to create a three-part model (see above). Tell the students to read their haiku aloud together several times. Then have them create a haiku scene by using the three-part model on the board. (List the parts on the board: 1. expressive speech only, 2. expressive speech and movement, 3. movement only, think the words.) Once everyone has memorized their haiku, have them practice their three ways of performing it. This task will take most groups about 10–15 minutes.

Invite students to get paper and art supplies from you (oil pastels, crayons, colored markers, chalk pastels, etc.) to draw a large scene or backdrop on butcher paper for their haiku performance. (Artwork will take an additional 15–20 minutes. Because of this time demand, you might consider completing it on another day.)

Finally, gather the class together to let them know they will be performing their haiku for each other. They will need a few minutes to revisit their movement/speech sequences. Let them know that each haiku group will unroll its "scenery" and will perform its haiku in three ways (point to the list on the board). End the performance with all the haiku groups performing their movement-only sequence at the same time. Use recorded music throughout the performance (adjusting volume during each group) and fade it out at the very end. Encourage the students to wait until the end of the performance to applaud.

EPISODE 2: BIOGRAPHY: THE LIFE AND POEMS OF THE MASTER HAIKU POET ISSA

Read aloud *Cool Melons—Turn to Frogs!: The Life and Poems of Issa* by Matthew Gollub. The text is the poignant story of Issa's life (1763-1827) interspersed with 33 examples of his haiku. The beautifully illustrated haiku become a central part of the storyline. If students prepared their performance (Episode #1) using one of Issa's haiku found within this book, let them say their particular haiku as it occurs in the story.

Script this book as a simple, dramatic Readers' Theatre presentation where several student narrators read the text of the story. Incorporate some of the student haiku performances (scenery and three-part speech/movement sequence) during several points in the dramatized Readers' Theatre. Perform for another class at your school.

EPISODE 3: WE ARE HAIKU POETS: EXTENSION PROJECTS FOR STUDENTS

Extensions for this unit could include the following learning activities:

➢ Write, illustrate, and perform original student haiku using the three-part model

➢ Create scenery and costumes for each haiku

➢ Create a photo essay to an original or traditional haiku

➢ Use student-created music compositions coordinated with haiku movements

> ➢ Create a haiku art gallery—display oil pastel or watercolor illustrations of student-created or traditional Japanese haiku
> ➢ Write in journals about haiku experiences

CONCLUSION

When our students are actively engaged in purposeful and expressive learning contexts that the arts can and do provide, haiku and other poetry comes alive in our classrooms. More important, both students and teachers become excited and recharged about the prospect of learning more poetry through these and other kinds of integrated activities. In my work within the San Diego State University City Heights Educational Collaborative's three urban schools (K–12), hundreds of students, teachers, and future teachers have been engaged through this successful haiku model.

Young students had much to say about what they learned. One student said, "We made the haiku come to life with what we saw in the poem." Another student seemed immersed in her haiku text and wrote, "In my haiku, I imagined that the water was so high up on my door that frogs were swimming. I made my haiku come to life by showing the frogs swimming. I also showed the rain pouring down. That's how I made my haiku, but I also used expression."

The many future teachers participating in the haiku study offered interesting perspectives about the unit. One future teacher reflected, "The words floated through the bodies of others like the haiku's spell had taken over them. I could see the words moving and taking shape before me." Another wrote:

> "Haiku is more than poetic words on a page. It involves something much deeper than simple, profound language. The *spirit* of the author comes alive when our imaginations take hold. We were able to not only hear the words, but also see the performers' interpretations and reactions. What a wonderful exercise to make poetry come alive."

Veteran classroom teachers also offered feedback. One teacher described her class's experiences by adding:

> "I imagine that this was the first opportunity most of my students have had to visualize poetry by using movement, speech, and art. What a powerful lesson! The students learned not only about Japanese culture and haiku, but also how to work in cooperative groups to create something on demand. Stu-

dents needed to use leadership skills, be willing to try something new, and perform in front of others despite any anxiety. This lesson reached all learners and caused students to synthesize their own poem to create art and vocal effects. They also used their visualization skills to make it come alive on paper and in the performance."

Finally, while providing creative, active learning opportunities for students within their study of haiku, we may be empowering more students to find meaning within poetic texts of all kinds. As Eric Jensen writes in *Arts with the Brain in Mind* (2001), "What we pay attention to increases our likelihood of remembering it" (p. 40). Let's continue to make haiku and other poetry memorable for all our students!

REFERENCES

Cox, C. (1998, April). *Children's stance towards literature: A longitudinal study, K–5.* Paper presented at the 1998 American Educational Research Association, San Diego.

Cox, C., & Many, J. E. (1992). Stance toward a literary work: Applying the transactional theory to children's responses. *Reading Psychology, 13,* 37–72.

Demi. (1992). *In the eyes of the cat.* New York: Holt.

Demi. (1993). *Demi's secret garden.* New York: Holt.

Gollub, M. (1998). *Cool melons—turn to frogs! The life and poems of Issa.* New York: Lee & Low.

Hancock, M. (2000). *A celebration of literature and response: Children, books, and teachers in the K–8 classrooms.* Upper Saddle River, NJ: Prentice Hall.

Jacobs, H. H. (1989). *Interdisciplinary curriculum: Design and implementation.* Alexandria, VA: Association for Supervision and Curriculum Development.

Jacobs, H. H. (1997). *Mapping the big picture: Integrating curriculum and assessment K–12.* Alexandria, VA: Association for Supervision and Curriculum Development.

Jensen, E. (2001). *Arts with the brain in mind.* Alexandria, VA: Association for Supervision and Curriculum Development.

Lapp, D., & Flood, J. (1992). *Teaching reading to every child* (3rd ed.). New York: Macmillan/McGraw-Hill.

McDonald, N., & Fisher, D. (1999). Living haiku: Scenes of sound in motion. In S. Totten, C. Johnson, L. R. Morrow, & T. Sills-Briegel (Eds.), *Practicing what we preach: Preparing middle level educators* (pp. 273–275). New York: Falmer.

McDonald, N., & Fisher, D. (2002). *Developing arts-loving readers: Top 10 questions teachers are asking about integrated arts education.* Lanham, MD: Scarecrow Education.

Rosenblatt, L. M. (1978). *The reader, the text, the poem: The transactional theory of the literary work.* Carbondale: Southern Illinois University Press.

Rosenblatt, L. M. (1995). *Literature as exploration*. New York: Modern Language Association.

Vygotsky, L. S. (1978). *Mind in society: The development of higher mental psychological processes*. Cambridge, MA: Harvard University Press.

Additional Resources for the Haiku Unit

Cassedy, S. (1992). *Red dragonfly on my shoulder*. New York: HarperCollins.

Hoobler, D. (1994). *Images across the ages: Japanese portraits*. Austin, TX: Raintree Steck-Vaughn.

Janeczko, P. (Ed.). (2000). *Stone bench in an empty park*. New York: Orchard.

Livingston, M. (1997). *Cricket never does: A collection of haiku and tanka*. New York: McElderry.

Spivak, D. (1997). *Grass sandals: The travels of Basho*. New York: Atheneum.

AMERICAN PANORAMAS
A Literature-Based Integrated Arts Curriculum Unit

I taste the ocean and wonder why it tastes like tears I sometimes cry.
—Ryan (2001)

I am the desert. I am free. Come walk the sweeping face of me.
—Siebert (1988)

I am the Heartland, great and wide. I sing of hope, I sing of pride.
—Siebert (1989)

As our students learn about America's geography and terrain, culture, and history, we want them to establish a meaningful understanding of the composition of our country's unique and varied landscapes. Experiences in which children are actively involved in creative response to children's literature about varied subject matter can create an engaging learning environment (Hancock, 2000). Creative movement, singing, musical listening, visual art, drama, and Readers' Theatre are all activities to be considered when planning instructional units in a variety of subject matter. The study of American terrain is no exception.

Unfortunately, some students have not been taught to think about the diversity in geography that the United States has to offer. Other students have learned about America's terrain from flat maps. We believe that students gain a deeper understanding of terrain when they experience it. However, we are realistic enough to know that we cannot fly students all over the country to experience terrain directly. Thankfully, students can gain a greater appreciation of the diversity of topography when they experience cultural artifacts that focus on terrain. As a fourth grade teacher noted after teaching her students about geography through the arts, "Understanding mountains for what they offer different groups of people was really good for my students. They used to believe that mountains were big rock piles."

The purpose of this appendix is to offer a direct model of an integrated arts curriculum unit featuring selected children's literature about American terrain: bodies of water (rivers, lakes, oceans, bays), deserts and canyons, mountains and forests, plains and valleys. Children's books and poetry will be paired with experiences for active reader response through singing, musical listening, movement, creative drama, Readers' Theatre, visual art, and performance. Within these varied literature-based learning activities, students will also explore factual content about American history, culture, and geography as related to terrain, specifically map reading, measurement (distance and time), altitude, climate, and indigenous flora and fauna. Students will work in both large group and small cooperative group settings. Finally, a resource list for classroom use is provided.

WHAT ARE THE ADVANTAGES OF INTEGRATING LEARNING ACTIVITIES USING THE ARTS INTO LANGUAGE ARTS AND OTHER SUBJECT AREAS?

If our goal is to increase children's learning through meaningful connections to the literature they are reading, we may need to explore a variety of contexts (including the arts) in which that learning may take place. Vygotsky (1978) argued that human language is developed through multiple signs, both verbal and nonverbal, during which learners connect learning to what they already know. Synthesis takes place through a child's active involvement with the meanings of language. Furthermore,

Integrative activities in which the arts' verbal and non-verbal communications and systems of thought are actively and creatively connected to learning within reading, writing, and oral language development can serve to heighten student interest and expressive involvement with learning at hand. By doing so, the arts are naturally connected to many subject areas. Purposeful integrated arts teaching contains many active avenues toward the literacy development of young readers (Hancock, 2000). By doing so, the arts can lend important experiences and context for language development. (McDonald & Fisher, 2002)

Albers (2001) investigated ways children demonstrate growth in literacy when "able to draw upon more than just written and oral language to create meaning" (p. 3). In her study, teachers and students actively connected the visual, dramatic, and musical arts with reading and writing activities tied to children's books. Learners were engaged in hands-on arts experiences in which they learned and used the multiple sign systems or literacies inherent in the arts. The students explored what it means to express themselves as artists (musicians, artists, actors) and create meaning through their active use of that art. The teachers in this study began to pay attention to how children make meaning and connections between print and nonprint communication. Albers summarized:

This knowledge enabled us, then, to draw from each of the sign systems to create multi-modal projects; to develop language arts curricula that depended on all sign systems to help children build their literacy; and to study, through children's artifacts, how children demonstrate growth in literacy and depth of response when able to draw upon more than just written and oral language to create meaning. (p. 3)

Through the use of a variety of arts-based activities tied to children's literature, students may directly experience a rich variety of avenues through which to interpret and communicate the meaning of what they are reading. Related art activity, dramatizations, Readers' Theatre, creative movement, song texts and music making, and other individual and cooperative group projects and performances can all be used to create a depth of experience to support children's literacy learning. To this, Albers concluded,

Although much of English/language arts instruction focuses on the development of children's linguistic skills, many scholars encourage language arts educators to broaden their scope of what constitutes language and meaning. These scholars argue that arts-based literacy instruction helps children solve problems in more complex ways (Gardner, 1991), enables them to communicate more deeply and richly (Harste, 1994) and allows them to engage in lively discussions and search for alternative perspectives. (Greene, 1995, cited in Albers, 2001, p. 9)

The following literature-based curriculum unit about American terrain involves active learning contexts within several subject areas, including social studies, language arts, science, and the arts. This integrated arts thematic unit is offered within five teaching episodes that may take place over several days or weeks of instruction in the general classroom. Additionally, a conceptual curriculum theme like American Panoramas might be adopted as a schoolwide theme for integrated instruction. Ideas for displays, student performances, and other extension activities are offered as ways for teachers to expand the use of thematic children's literature within the larger school learning environment.

MODEL UNIT ON AMERICAN "PANORAMAS"

The activities outlined in this curriculum unit can be taught over several class sessions. Depending on the amount of time a teacher can devote to the study of terrain per day, this unit may last between 5 and 12 days. We do suggest, however, that the following episodes be taught in order.

Episode 1: Background Knowledge

In order to introduce students to the concept of terrain, share the book *I Love the Mountains* (Archambault & Plummer, 1999). Students must be immediately involved in active learning experiences that use vocabulary about terrains. This book will likely motivate students to learn more about this topic. The first verse of this book is based on a song (see Table E.1). Students can learn to sing this verse from the CD recording. Another song text book, *This Land is Your Land* (Guthrie, 1998), can be shared with students as they sing the song with or without the CD recording (available in *Making Music*, 2002, grade 5, p. 116, CD 5-13).

After sharing these books, engage the students in a discussion about the types of terrain: What kinds of terrain are there (deserts, mountains and forests, canyons, bodies of water, plains and valleys, etc.)? How many different kinds of terrain are within our own city or town? List locations of local terrain. Within 100 miles? Within our state? Where are they? Describe these land features and find them on maps.

There are many key vocabulary words that are introduced in these two texts. The teacher should create a word list for students to study as they learn more about terrain in this unit. For example, students should know the following words: redwood forest, Gulf stream waters, Rockies, lakes, plains, desert, redwood firs, Mount Rushmore, Niagara Falls, Grand Canyon, and Lady Liberty. The last page of *I Love the Mountains* has a wonderful map of the United States with significant terrains identified that could be used in a map location activity.

To ensure that students focus their learning on these and other vocabulary words, we suggest using vocabulary cards with the following features:

Word	Definition of the word
Illustration of the word	Sentence containing the word

TABLE E.1. Teaching Resources for American Panoramas Unit

Type of terrain	Children's literature	Songs	Musical listening
Bodies of water	Locker, T. (1997). *Water dance.* New York: Harcourt. (poetic text)	"Roll on Columbia" (grade 5, p. 114, CD 5-11)	*The Moldau* from *Ma Vlast* by Smetana (classical orchestra)
	Ryan, P. (2001). *Hello ocean.* Watertown, MA: Charlesbridge.	"Erie Canal" (grade 5, p. 254, CD 10-7)	"The River Suite: Finale" by Virgil Thomson (grade 5, CD 5-16)
	Seymour, S. (1990). *Oceans.* New York: HarperCollins.	"Mississippi River Chant" (grade 2, p. 130, CD 4-33)	"Shenandoah" (grade 2, CD 2-29; grade 5 CD 10-12)
	Siebert, D. (2001). *Mississippi.* New York: HarperCollins.	"Rio Grande" (grade 4, p. 250, CD 9-6)	"Tennessee River" by Randy Owen (grade 5, CD 13-21)
	Simon, S. (1990). *Oceans.* New York: Morrow.	"Shenandoah" (grade 5, p. 256, CD 10-10)	
	Zolotow, C. (1992). *The seashore book.* New York: HarperCollins.	"Beach Rap" (speech piece) (grade 1, p. 336, CD 9-29)	
		"From Sea to Shining Sea" (grade 2, p. 330, CD 11-11)	
Canyons and deserts	Baylor, B. (1993). *Desert voices.* New York: Aladdin.	"Mos, Mos" (Hopi) (grade 1, p. 130, CD 3-52)	"Death Valley Suite: Desert Water Hole" by Ferde Grofé (grade 8, CD 8-17)
	Cameron, E. (2002). *Canyon.* New York: Mikaya Press.	"I Walk in Beauty" (Navajo) (grade 4, p. 272, CD 10-3)	"Grand Canyon Suite: Cloudburst" by Ferde Grofé (K, CD 8-23)
	Lesser, C. (1997). *Storm on the desert.* New York: Harcourt.		"Watchers of the Canyon" by Burning Sky (grade 6, CD 11-9)
	Seymour, S. (1990). *Deserts.* New York: Mulberry.		"Daybreak Vision" by R. Carlos Nakai (Native American Flute) (grade 5, CD 15-19)
	Siebert, D. (1988). *Mojave.* New York: HarperCollins.		
	Simon, S. (1997). *Deserts.* New York: Mulberry.		

Mountains and forests	Locker, T. (2001). *Mountain dance.* New York: Harcourt. Seymour, S. (1994). *Mountains.* New York: Mulberry. Siebert, D. (1991). *Sierra.* New York: HarperCollins. Simon, S. (1997). *Mountains.* New York: Mulberry.	"Tall Cedar Tree" (grade 2, p. 310, CD 10-21) "The Tree in the Wood" (grade 2, p. 346, CD 12-1) "I Love the Mountains" (grade 5, p. 34, CD 2-11) "My Home's Across the Blue Ridge Mountains" (grade 4, p. 82, CD 3-43) "Scurwood Mountain" (grade 4, p. 63, CD 3-5)	"Stopping by Woods on a Snowy Evening" (recorded poetry by Robert Frost) (grade 6, p. 44, CD 2-30, 2-31) "Ozark Mountain Jubilee" Murah/Anders (grade 4, CD 3-45) "This Land Is Your Land" by Woody Guthrie (grade 5, CD 5-15)
Plains and valleys	Bouchard, D. (1995). *If you're not from the prairie.* New York: Atheneum. Fowler, A. (2000). *Living on the plains.* New York: Children's Press. Hundal, N. (1999). *Prairie summer.* New York: Fitzhenry and Whiteside, Ltd. Siebert, D. (1989). *Heartland.* New York: HarperCollins.	"Bury Me Not on the Lone Prairie" (grade 6, p. 11, CD 1-6) "Cattle Call" (grade 5, p. 332, CD 13-16) "El Rancho Grande" (grade 4, p. 211 CD 7-40) "Home on the Range" (grade 5, p. 68, CD 3-27) "Streets of Laredo" (grade 5, p. 10, CD 9-21) "Oklahoma" (grade 5, p. 36, CD 2-14) "Route 66" (grade 4, p. 266, CD 9-24)	"Route 66" by Bobby Troup (grade 4, CD 9-27) "Cattle Call" by Tex Owens (grade 5, CD 13-18)

Note. Songs and most Musical Listening resources are from *Making Music* (K–8 National Text Series in Music) © 2002, Pearson Education/Scott Foresman, Silver Burdett Music

These 5" × 7" cards can also be used as homework. Our experience suggests that students should complete the top two sections (the word and its definition) and then complete the remaining two sections at home.

Episode 2: Group Poem "American Panoramas"

Photocopy the poem in Table E.2 onto an overhead. The teacher should read this poem aloud to the class while they read it silently from the overhead. Immediately following the teacher reading, the poem should be read aloud again. This time, all of the students and the teacher should choral read the poem aloud together. The poem's stanzas will be later used in small group tasks and within a large group performance using creative movement and art.

Add the new vocabulary, such as New England, the Mississippi Delta, and Monument Valley from the "American Panoramas" poem to the terrain word list. In addition, ask students to create vocabulary cards for these new words.

Trace the route of the poem on a map of the United States. The teacher may ask each student to find one specific location in his or her individual atlas. Then the teacher may ask each student to come to the large map in the front of the room and trace the route that the poem identifies. Extension activities involve examining the distance traveled between points mentioned in the poem as well as finding photos of these locales in books and on the Internet.

Episode 3: Pop-Up Facts about Terrain

Using a social studies textbook, photographs, posters, slides, and illustrations, the teacher shows the students pictures of different types of terrain. Pop-up facts are created, one for each student, based on snippets of factual information about terrain. For example, pop-up fact about mountains may include the following:

➤ Most mountains are formed when plates—giant pieces of the Earth's crust—push and pull against each other.

➤ Some mountains are formed when rocks pull apart or break.

➤ Some mountains are formed by volcanic eruptions.

Obviously the teacher would display different pictures for each of these particular pop-up facts.

When the teacher displays the visual of a certain type of terrain (e.g., canyons), the students with pop-up facts about canyons will stand (one at a time) and individually read their information about that terrain as the class listens and looks at the visual. The visuals of terrain could be arranged so that all the facts about one

TABLE E.2. Group Poem

"American Panoramas"
by Nan McDonald

America stretches from sea to sea, from east to west, and north to south
Over plains and valleys, deserts and canyons, mountains and forests,
Her rivers and lakes are our constant companions
As we celebrate our land's designs
A panorama of places come to mind . . .

(Water)
From craggy coasts of New England's Atlantic shore
Down to the Chesapeake Bay and crabs galore
To Carolina's Outer Banks and Florida Keys' sparkling sand
On to the Gulf shore where hurricanes can meet land

Up the Mississippi Delta, we meet the Ohio and Missouri
Where we could travel to five Great Lakes, if we weren't in such a hurry.
A plane trip west and we could boast
Of the incredible beauty of our Pacific Northwest Coast.

Southward to Oregon and California's Golden shore,
A bay surrounds San Francisco, known for bridges and more,
Near the famous Hearst Castle, sea otters swim and play.
Southern California's beaches are just a dream away.

(Deserts and canyons)
As we leave the West Coast and travel east
On great deserts our eyes will feast
Where the Colorado slowly carved the Grand Canyon of color,
Bryce Canyon and Zion are part of the lore.

The great American desert has its own Monument Valley
Where spires and mesas are too many to tally
The desert's a kingdom of sand and heat
With unusual sites that can't be beat.

(Forests and mountains)
The Sierra, Cascades, Rocky Mountains are here
Formed by volcanoes or glaciers, it's clear
Covered with forests of aspen and pine
Where streams melt into rivers that flow throughout time

Pioneers crossed great mountains seeking fortunes of gold
Instead they found great hardships, we are told.
The mountains were crossed to build this great nation
Their journeys provide food for our imagination

(Plains and valleys)
Eastward again over seas of grass, corn, and wheat
The Great Plains provide food for Americans to eat
The golden land rolls gently over hills, valleys, and more
Adding to America's Panorama from shore to shore.

Where herds of bison once roamed the free range
And drank at her rivers which have seen much change
Great cities and towns have kept America strong
May we always be free and our people live long.

(All)
America—a Panorama of great beauty
The care of the earth must be our first duty
We want our children to see this terrain
So caring for the earth will be our refrain.

terrain are given in succession, or different types of visuals of terrains could be mixed up so students begin to see the differences between them. The pop-up cards could also be numbered so that the teacher simply mentions a number and the student with that card reads his or her information.

This particular activity allows students to practice their oral language skills. As most adults know, speaking in front of peers can be terrifying. This activity provides students with practice in doing so.

Episode 4: Learning Centers

Learning centers allow groups of students to develop expertise about terrain. The activities suggested in this episode may take place over three or more class periods. We suggest that students be placed in four groups. Each of the groups will be assigned a center based on one of the following terrain groups: water (rivers, lakes, oceans), canyons and deserts, mountains, and plains and valleys. When students arrive at their center they will find CDs, informational books about that terrain, children's literature and poetry about that terrain, social studies texts, art supplies, maps, atlas, etc.

A number of tasks should take place at each center. We suggest the following:

1. Learn a song about that terrain and create an illustrated book using that song's text. Songs can be learned from CD recordings of the selections in Table E.1 and students may listen on headphones using a multi-output player (listening station). Students should read along with the song from the music textbook, trade book, or other printed material. Songs may be performed for the whole class during episode 5.

2. Read selected texts at the center about the terrain (see Table E.1). After independently reading these books and discussing them with members of the group, students should create a readers' guide with three questions for other students to answer when they later visit that center. For example, questions from the mountain center may include: Where are the largest mountains in the United States? Who tried to cross the Sierra Mountains? To get to the Gold Rush in California, what mountains did prospectors have to cross?

3. Create a poster or montage of the terrain on butcher paper using torn paper, magazine illustrations and photographs, and original drawings of that type of terrain. Students should find a poem selection or descriptive phrases from the books they have read at the center and write them on their poster. Students should also label examples of where that terrain is found in America and

use terms and vocabulary about that terrain in the writing on the poster. Finally, students could include information about the flora and fauna of the terrain.

4. After the students have completed tasks 1–3, they may work together to create a movement sequence to perform. This performance should be based on the stanzas of the group poem "American Panoramas" appropriate to their terrain.

Episode 5: Performance Sharing

The final episode includes opportunities for students to share what they have learned about terrain with their peers. We suggest creating a number of informal opportunities, including:

➤ A class performance of the "American Panoramas" poem featuring each terrain group's creative movement and art during their stanzas.

➤ Students visits the three other terrain centers. Students focus on the readers' guide created by the original group and answer the questions using the texts at the center. They may also listen to songs about that terrain, but may not have time to create a poster or another movement sequence for the group poem.

➤ Invite another class or parent group to visit one or more of the terrain centers and view the group performance of the "American Panoramas" poem.

CONCLUSION

Students are often engaged in the study of geography as passive readers of informational texts. However, this does not often produce real learning or interest. We suggest that informational texts can be easily supplemented with children's literature, songs, poems, creative movement, and visual art about terrain. Furthermore, students can be actively involved in creative activities and performances that allow them opportunities to express the meaning of what they are reading. In this way, the study of terrain is more than a passing interest. Rather, it becomes a way of thinking about the world in which they live.

REFERENCES

Albers, P. (2001). Literacy in the arts. *Primary Voices K–6, 9*(4), 3–9.

Archambault, J., & Plummer, D. R. (1999). *I love the mountains*. Parsippany, NJ: Silver Press.

Gardner, H. (1991). *The unschooled mind: How children think and how schools should teach.* New York: Basic Books.

Greene, M. (1995). *Releasing the imagination: Essays on education, the arts, and social change.* San Francisco: Jossey-Bass.

Guthrie, W. (1998). *This land is your land.* New York: Little, Brown.

Hancock, M. (2000). *A celebration of literature and response: Children, books, and teachers in the K–8 classrooms.* Upper Saddle River, NJ: Prentice Hall.

Harste, J. C. (1994). Literacy as curricular conversations about knowledge, inquiry, and morality. In R. B. Ruddell, M. R. Ruddell, & H. Singer (Eds.), *Theoretical models and processes of reading* (pp. 1220-1242). Newark, DE: International Reading Association.

McDonald, N., & Fisher, D. (2002). *Developing arts loving readers: Top ten questions teachers are asking about integrated arts education.* Lanham, MD: Scarecrow Press.

Ryan, P. M. (2001). *Hello ocean.* Watertown, MA: Charlesbridge.

Siebert, D. (1988). *Mojave.* New York: HarperTrophy.

Siebert, D. (1989). *Heartland.* New York: HarperTrophy.

Vygotsky, L. S. (1978). *Mind in society: The development of higher mental psychological processes.* Cambridge, MA: Harvard University Press.

JAZZ LISTENING ACTIVITIES
Children's Literature and Authentic Music Samples

> I keep wondering if I don't need to do a lot more introductory listening lessons involving jazz and even the stories of jazz musicians. Even though I am really limited in my own background about jazz, I still know it's just not enough to have my kids play or sing a simple blues scale and listen to one or two old standards! How can I make jazz really mean something to kids?
>
> —Veteran general music teacher

Many of us have tremendous natural passion and empathy for jazz. We know that jazz holds a respected place within a comprehensive general music curriculum—a curriculum that includes active student listening experiences to authentic sources of the genre, accurately set within the rich historical and cultural contexts in which the music was and is created (MENC, 1994). Some important questions begin to emerge: What is it about jazz that excites us? Is it the unique combinations of musical sound or is it the improvisations that intrigue us? More important, how can we share our excitement about this American music with our students? How can we encourage them to learn about the rich historical and artistic contexts in which unique personalities created and still create jazz?

One way to establish heightened student interest in listening to many styles of jazz is through the use of children's books about jazz and its artists. While fiction-alized accounts are interesting and important in many units of study, the study of jazz provides students an interesting opportunity to learn through another curricu-

From *Music Educators Journal,* 89(2), 43–49, 57. Copyright 2002. Adapted by permission of MENC: The National Association for Music Education.

lum genre—biography. Reading biographies provides students with an authentic glimpse inside history and encourages them to understand historical events from the perspective of people who lived it (Moyers, 2000).

Furthermore, classroom learning activities in which biographies are paired with authentic music listening samples from appropriate jazz artists may serve to enhance student learning. These kinds of purposeful instructional pairings can "emphasize relationships among the arts and relationships between the arts and disciplines outside the arts. Music can serve as a particularly useful framework within which to teach a wide array of skills and knowledge, particularly in social studies and language arts" (MENC, 1994, p. 4). As an added bonus, the natural integrative learning connections between these kinds of musical learning experiences and students' literacy development can easily be established and articulated to others at school sites, thereby strengthening the important role of music within the larger school curriculum (Fisher, McDonald, & Strickland, 2001).

We offer a teaching model and suggestions for teachers to create active introductory listening experiences for upper elementary and middle school students paired with engaging biographies about jazz and jazz artists. Included are activities and resources about pre-jazz forms and musicians (West African influences, work songs, spirituals, ragtime, New Orleans jazz, early blues, etc.), jazz (swing, scat, bebop, cool, hard bop, post bop, avant garde, etc.), and jazz musicians, as well as popular styles of music derived from jazz (rhythm and blues, soul, funk, fusion jazz rock, Latin jazz, rap, hip hop, etc.).

Student activities within this model curriculum unit include:

➤ Listening to, identifying, analyzing, responding to, and reflecting upon various styles of pre-jazz and jazz (National Standards 6, 7, 9)

➤ Identification of the instruments, vocal and instrumental techniques, and style characteristics used in various types of jazz and related forms by sound and sight (National Standard 6)

➤ Active musical listening within historically accurate settings (set within children's literature contexts), which are used to increase student understanding of the chronological development of jazz through learning about the times, lives, and works of its artists (National Standards 6, 7, 8)

➤ Awareness of eras of history and culture, including West African musical influences on roots of jazz (pre-jazz) found within slavery experiences of African Americans, and development of vocabulary and understanding of the historical and cultural contexts of jazz reflected in visual art, photography, poetry, and biography of selected artists and their music (National Standards 8, 9)

> Student learning through reading and directed writing experiences, including small group cooperative learning activity, student poetry, journals, illustrated student books, and bulletin boards based on musical listening activities paired with children's literature about pre-jazz, jazz, and musicians (National Standards 6, 7, 8, 9)

> Created movement, visual art, and drama used in informal performance sharing about jazz artists and music (National Standards 6, 7, 8)

In addition to offering model curriculum and performance ideas, this article provides lists of jazz listening resources, children's literature about jazz, video resources, and resources for teaching about jazz.

MODEL TEACHING UNIT

This listening unit, Introduction to Jazz, is organized into five episodes. Each of these episodes is a stage of the unit and may require between one and four class sessions, depending on the amount of time a teacher may choose to focus on jazz and its artists. These episodes include suggestions for extended student learning through partnerships with classroom teachers who may be interested in the small group cooperative learning processes and performances described below. Thus, this unit allows music classroom activities to become a focus within language arts instruction. Sources include materials appropriate for grades 4–8.

Event 1

To introduce this unit, show pictures of a wide variety of instruments common to jazz as well as pictures of jazz musicians. For background music, use one of the listening selections from Table F.1. Video sources listed in Table F.2 may also be used to set the scene. Engage students in a preliminary class discussion using some of the following questions as student responses are listed on the board: What is jazz? Who plays jazz? Where did it come from? How old is it? Is jazz heard today? Where? Begin creating a class list of words that are used to describe jazz and keep this posted word list handy for further reference and revision as needed.

Following this class discussion, introduce the book *The Jazz Fly* (Gollub, 2000). This book contains a CD recording that is an exact replica of the text,

TABLE F.1. Suggested Jazz Listening Samples

Jazz style[a]	Artist/recording	Elements/notes
Origins: African influences (pre-jazz)	African Tribal Music and Dances (Legacy International) CD-308 SBG-Video (grade 6—dancing) and (grade 2—rhythm) "Compagnons D'Akati-Cote d'Ivorire (Ivory Coast Drummers and Dancers)," (grade 4—percussion) "Dou Dou Rose Ensemble-Senegal"	Listen for polyphonic and layered rhythms, ostinati patterns, indigenous percussion, African vocal styles. Add visual elements provided in these videos to increase students' understanding of percussion instruments, characteristics of the music, and its links to rhythmic dance.
Songs of Slavery (pre-jazz)	"Follow the Drinkin' Gourd" SBG-TMC (grade 3, CD 6-26) "Oh, Freedom" SBG-MM (grade 5, CD 15-17) "Everytime I Feel the Spirit" SBG-MM (grade 5, CD 9-23) SBG-Video (grade 3—One Voice, Many Voices) "Great Gettin' Up Morning"	Expressive vocal solo/choral style related to later developments in gospel music. Use of solo/refrain, syncopation.
Ragtime (pre-jazz)	Scott Joplin: "The Entertainer" SBG-TMC (grade 7, CD 3-23) "Maple Leaf Rag" SBG-TMC (grade 3, CD 1-15) "Cotton Ball Rag" and "New Rag" SBG-MM (grade 5, CD 13-3 & 13-6)	Joplin considered his music classical. Notice the absence of improvisation in these compositions. The left hand lends rhythmic harmonic support; the right hand offers syncopated rhythm and chord figures.
Birth of the Blues Part one	Huddie Ledbetter: "Shorty George" SBG-TMC (grade 7, CD 8-4) "Good Mornin' Blues" SBG-MM (grade 5, CD 9-3) Muddy Waters: Bottleneck Guitar "Country Blues" SBG-MM (grade 5, CD 9-5) Robert Johnson: "Walkin' Blues" SBG-MM (grade 5, CD 9-6)	African vocal style applied to jazz, pitch bending, scoops, rasping, etc. Early blues style is the foundation of modern rhythm and blues. Listen for the storytelling nature of the blues lyrics.

		African vocal style applied to early blues genre.
Birth of the Blues Part two (This style is directly tied to early jazz [New Orleans, 1920s]).	Bessie Smith: "St. Louis Blues" SBG-MM (grade 5, CD 14-3) "Lost Your Head Blues" *Smithsonian Collection of Classic Jazz, Volume 1*, track 3 and 4	
Jazz Beginnings (New Orleans jazz)	Original Dixieland Jazz Band: "Dixie Jazz Band One Step" (First recording of instrumental jazz, distributed February, 1917) *Jazz Classics Compact Disc/Jazz Styles: History and Analysis* Compiled and Annotated by Mark C. Gridley, track 7	This performance also exemplifies the common New Orleans horn line-up of cornet, clarinet, and trombone. The horns play in a polyphonic style. The rhythm section consists of only piano and drums.
	Louis Armstrong: "Hotter than That" SBG-MM (grade 5, CD 3-20)	Listen for Armstrong's trumpet solo and improvised singing (scat solo) with guitar accompaniment.
	Jelly Roll Morton: "Black Bottom Stomp" (1926), *Smithsonian Collection of Classic Jazz, Volume 1*, track 6	Listen for the three-horn front line and the rhythm section including string bass and banjo. Morton's unaccompanied piano solo uses syncopation similar to Joplin's "Maple Leaf Rag" with the added swing feel unique to jazz.
Sounds of the Swing Era (Late 1920s–'40s)	Duke Ellington: "It Don't Mean a Thing (If You Ain't Got That Swing)" with Ella Fitzgerald, SBG-MM (grade 5, CD 3-8)	Listen for the walking bassline, which is the foundation of the swing rhythmic feel. Also notice the short solo improvisations woven into the fabric of the arrangement. Note the use of the plunger mute on the trombone solo played as if speaking to the musical listeners.
	"Harlem Airshaft," *Duke Ellington and the Blanton-Webster Band* (RCA 5659-2-RB) track 15, and "Ko Ko," track 3	Listen for the smooth melodic style and drummer Gene Krupa's driving beat on the bass drum.
	Benny Goodman: "Sing, Sing, Sing," *Live at Carnegie Hall: 1938* (Sony/Columbia)	Goodman heard with Count Basie. Drummer Joe Jones's style here is an interesting contrast to Krupa's style as he de-emphasizes the bass drum and instead uses the swing ride pattern on the high-hat cymbals.
	Benny Goodman with Charlie Christian and Count Basie: "I Found a New Baby," *Smithsonian Collection of Classic Jazz, Volume 2*, track 23	

(cont.)

TABLE F.1. (cont.)

Jazz style[a]	Artist/recording	Elements/notes
Jazz Women	**Ella Fitzgerald:** "How High the Moon" (1961) SBG-MM (grade 5, CD 13-13)	Vocal improvisation in the scat style of jazz instrumentalists. In this performance, Fitzgerald quotes a number of well-known tunes and weaves them into her melodic improvisations.
	Sarah Vaughn: "My Funny Valentine" (1973), *Smithsonian Collection of Classic Jazz, Volume 4*, track 5	Listen for the ballad style with piano. Sung in a *rubato* feel, or with the absence of a steady tempo, freely interpreted lyrics and melody.
	Diane Schuur, Jazz Vocalist: SBG-Video: (grade 4, singing styles)	Video performance of varying jazz vocal styles.
	Some important innovative jazz women (composers, arrangers, and performers) from 1970 to present are:	
	Carla Bley	
	Jane Ira Bloom	
	Geri Allen	
	Maria Schneider	
Bebop Jazz (1940s)	**Charlie Parker:** "Now is the Time" SBG-MM (grade 5, CD 15-25)	Parker, along with Dizzy Gillespie, changed the direction and future of jazz with brilliant innovations. Listen for Parker's lucid improvisation over a walking bassline and how the drums interact rhythmically with Parker.
	Theolonius Monk: "Bemsha Swing," *Brilliant Corners* (Riverside OJCD-026-2)	Monk's compositional style ran counter to the majority of his peers and featured unusual chords and rhythms. Listen for the timpani solo from drummer Max Roach.
Cool Jazz (from 1946)	**Miles Davis:** "Boplicity" (1949), *Smithsonian Collection of Classic Jazz, Volume 4*, track 1	Features the more subdued and cerebral, relaxed sound of cool. Listen for the unusual blend of brass including French horn and tuba with alto and baritone saxes.
Hard Bop (early 1950s)	**Horace Silver and the Jazz Messengers:** "The Preacher" (1955) (Blue Note, CD P 7 46140 2), track 6	Hard bop follows on the heels of cool jazz as a reaction to its subdued nature. Strong blues flavor of theme and solos is paired here with a more aggressive rhythmic feel.

178

Post Bop (1960s)	Miles Davis: "So What" from *Kind of Blue* (1959) (Columbia-CK 64935), track 1 John Coltrane: "Impressions" from *Live at the Village Vanguard* (1961) (Impulse AS 10), track 3	Post bop chronologically follows after hard bop and focus is off harmonic progressions toward more modal structures. Call-and-response melody line. Davis uses silence during his solo trumpet line. Coltrane's more dense solo style is emotionally intense in tempo and energy.)
Avant Garde (Modern/experimental)	Ornette Coleman: "Lonely Woman" (1959), *Smithsonian Collection of Classic Jazz, Volume 5*, track 7	A challenge for young listeners! This abstract form features improvised jazz structures as well as melodies. Bass and a driving, fast tempo are paired with trumpet and alto sax in their unrelated, slower tempi, creating a mournful, distinctive sound.
Gospel	Take Six: "Get Away Jordan" (1988) (Reunion 7001 0032726), track 7	This vocal group effectively swings without the help of a rhythm section. Listen for the challenging and sophisticated gospel arrangements.
Rhythm & Blues/Soul	James Brown: *Foundations of Funk* (United Artists/Verve) Aretha Franklin: *Lady Soul* (Atlantic/Rhino)	Listeners will recognize these great artists as the original Godfather and Queen of Soul. Listen for the driving bass and solo with call and response.
Funk	Herbie Hancock: "Watermelon Man" SBG-TMC (grade 7, CD 6-13) Kool and the Gang: "Spirit of the Boogie" (United Artists/Mercury) Tower of Power: "Back to Oakland" on *Tower of Power Greatest Hits* (Sony/Columbia)	Let the students articulate what they hear. Driving bass beat? Solos? Improvisations?
Fusion (Jazz rock)	Weather Report: "Birdland" from *Heavy Weather* (Columbia)	Guide attention to the creative manner in which keyboardist Joseph Zawinul uses synthesizers to create different colors and textures in the music.

(cont.)

179

TABLE F.1. *(cont.)*

Jazz style[a]	Artist/recording	Elements/notes
Latin Jazz	Salsa: Eddie Palmieri "Palmas" (Wea/Elektra) Brazilian Samba: Chick Corea "Spain" from *Light as a Feather* (United Artists/Verve) Brazilian Bossa Nova: Getz and Astrud Gilberto "Girl from Ipanema" (United Artists)	Highly syncopated music. Listen for timbales and congas as primary percussion instruments. Contrast these two samples with the more well-known Salsa styles. These Brazilian forms feature Portuguese and English lyrical melodies with improvisation.
Rap/Hip Hop	Let your students advise you further here. Suggestions: "The Message" by Grandmaster Flash and the Furious Five "Africa's Inside Me" by Arrested Development	Encourage students to listen with their "musical" ears rather than merely to decipher "whether or not you like this music." Ask students to use musical terms and listening checklist items as they analyze and discuss more popular and well-known styles of music.

Several listening samples listed here are from the K–8 basal text series in Music—*The Music Connection* © 1995, 2000, and/or *Making Music* © 2002 by Silver Burdett and Ginn, Pearson Education/Scott Foresman Publishers, Parsippany, New Jersey. Abbreviations are as follows: SBG-TMC (*The Music Connection*) and SBG-MM (*Making Music*). Also referenced is the SBG video series, "Music Magic:Video Library," abbreviated as SBG-Video.

[a]Jazz style categories and chronological order correspond to pre-jazz and jazz styles, and styles of music related to jazz as mentioned within in the children's books *I See the Rhythm* by Toyomi Igus and Michele Wood (Children's Book Press, 1998) and *The Sound That Jazz Makes* by Carole Boston Weatherford (Walker and Company, 2000).

TABLE F.2. Videos about Jazz

Early blues: *Bluesland: Portrait in American Music* (Masters of American Music Videos)[a]

Louis Armstrong: *Satchmo* (Masters of American Music Videos)[a]

Duke Ellington: *On the Road with Duke Ellington* (The Robert Drew Archive)[a]

Duke Ellington and His Orchestra, 1929–1943[*]

Ella Fitzgerald: *Ella Fitzgerald, Something to Live For*[*]

Sarah Vaughn: *Sarah Vaughn, The Divine One* (Masters of American Music Videos)[a]

Billie Holiday: *Billie Holiday, The Many Faces of Lady Day* (Masters of American Music Videos)[a]

Miles Davis: *Miles Ahead: The Music of Miles Davis*[b]

Miles in Paris[b]

John Coltrane: *John Coltrane Jazz Casual with Ralph J. Gleason*[*]

The World According to John Coltrane[*]

Thelonious Monk: *Thelonious Monk, American Composer*[b]

Monk in Oslo[b]

[a]Available from The Jazz Store (800-558-9513 or www.thejazzstore.com).
[b]Available from Jamey Abersold's 2001 Jazz Catalog (800-456-1388).

including the scat sounds and instruments. Following this shared reading experience, invite students to discuss jazz and how the music is made. Include questions such as: What instruments are used in jazz? Why did the fly want a new sound? Why are nonsense words sung during the music? Do other kinds of music sound like this? Add students' ideas to the word list.

As this discussion closes, introduce the book *The Sound that Jazz Makes* (Weatherford, 2000). Invite different groups of students expressively to read aloud this book's poetic 2-page text spreads, which are organized to reflect the chronological history and development of jazz. During each group's read-aloud, play recorded segments of the appropriate jazz style (mentioned within the book's text) found in selections from Table F.1. Allow time during each group's read-aloud for students to hear little of each of these selections as they see or are shown the book's excellent illustrations. Following this first event, students are interested in jazz and motivated to learn more about it.

Event 2

This stage of instruction is an outgrowth of students' interest in understanding jazz and jazz musicians. Event 2 activities are concerned with active listening and student analysis of that listening based on learning about the chronological, historical development of jazz found in the book *I See the Rhythm* (Igus, 1998). The book's highly engaging text was written and illustrated as a listening response to jazz of many styles. In addition, *I See the Rhythm* includes a chronological jazz timeline in the margins of each page of text.

Once again, invite small groups of students expressively to read aloud pages on which each style of jazz is presented (e.g., jazz beginnings, sounds of swing, blues, etc.). Again, use this literature activity as an opportunity to pair student read-alouds with style-appropriate listening samples and/or video viewing suggestions from Tables F.1 and F.2. Recorded music provides a great way musically to introduce each group's poetic read-aloud about a particular period of jazz while allowing listeners added opportunities to hear the musical sample during and after each poem. Although this type of scripted listening activity takes a bit of time and preparation, its purposeful pairing of expressive speech with authentic listening samples of the period can provide a highly engaging and effective musical learning environment.

After these activities, students may be both curious and ready to understand more about the historical development of jazz. It may be helpful to create a classroom jazz timeline by using butcher paper that is between 6 and 9 feet long and has sections mapped off and labeled by separate eras and styles of jazz. The jazz timeline should remain on the wall throughout this unit (along with the class list of words to describe jazz) as students will be updating these displays as they complete their studies of jazz.

Event 3

Activities in this event are designed to increase further students' understanding of jazz through active listening, analysis, identification, and vocabulary development. The Listening to Jazz Checklist (Table F.3) should be introduced to students as a classification system and an eventual assessment tool. Many of the words found on the word list created in events 1 and 2 are likely to be found on the checklist (e.g., improv, tempo, instrumentation, rhythm section, etc.). This checklist contains many of the common terms used to discuss jazz. Teachers may want to customize their own checklist for classroom use based on the recordings and vocabulary they intend to use.

Select several jazz recordings and invite students to listen to them. As they listen, guide students in how to use the checklist as they make individual and large group decisions about what they are hearing. Use an overhead transparency to discuss the student selections in each column. For instance, if the dynamics in a recorded selection frequently change, invite students to describe these changes in their own words. Once students have been guided through several episodes of using the Listening to Jazz Checklist, invite them to analyze new (not previously heard) jazz listening samples and apply their knowledge. Students could also work in teams or small cooperative groups during the checklist activity and write their

TABLE F.3. Listening to Jazz Checklist

Instruments	Rhythm section	Style	Tempo	Dynamics	Improv	Artist name
☐ Piano	☐ Walking bassline	☐ Pre-Jazz (West African, work songs, spirituals, New Orleans, ragtime)	☐ Fast	☐ Loud	☐ Solo	☐ _____
☐ Bass	☐ Pattern on high hat	☐ Early Blues	☐ Medium	☐ Medium	☐ Solo within the group	☐ _____
☐ Drums	☐ Chatter on snare	☐ Blues (country blues, delta blues guitar, others)	☐ Slow	☐ Soft	☐ Solo with rhythm section	☐ _____
☐ Assorted percussion	☐ Others:	☐ Chicago Stride	☐ Fast to slow	☐ Changing (how?)	☐ Playing in the moment (all improvised)	
☐ Sax		☐ Swing (vocal/instrumental)	☐ Slow to fast			
☐ Clarinet		☐ Scat	☐ Changes (how?)			
☐ Other winds		☐ Bebop				
☐ Guitar		☐ Fusion				
☐ Electronic or computerized		☐ Funk				
☐ Others:		☐ Latin jazz				
		☐ Others:				

183

answers on overhead transparencies or on large poster-size papers to be shared with the larger group. Varying the task each time will increase student interest and motivation.

At the conclusion of this event, invite students to add titles of jazz recordings and the artist's name to the classroom jazz timeline. For instance, students might add the title "St. Louis Blues," written by W. C. Handy and performed by Bessie Smith, to the timeline under the era "Birth of the Blues."

Event 4

No study of jazz would be complete without learning about its artists and their music-making styles. The activities in this event involve a biography study through cooperative learning and creative presentations about jazz and jazz musicians and will likely take several class periods. These suggestions are meant to model the breadth of possible activities that could be included to help students understand the complexity of artists and the times in which they lived. Table F.4 provides a list of possible jazz artists to study as well as a number of quality biographical books currently available.

In this activity, called "Getting to Know Jazz Musicians," small groups of four to six students should be assigned an artist to study. Time should be provided for students to find and read books or websites about their artist. Students should be provided time to work in small cooperative learning groups (panels) to create a presentation for the whole class or another class. This presentation may be presented in four parts.

Part 1: All about Our Artist

The goal for part 1 is to connect the biography study to understanding about jazz and jazz musicians. Students should be reminded to focus on key aspects of their artist—aspects that everyone in the class needs to know about. Biographies and other materials about selected jazz artists and their music should be provided for the students to research in the music classroom, library, or general classroom.

Each group should be provided with space on a class bulletin board or large poster for the opening portion of their presentation, entitled "We Learned about _____." During this part of the presentation, students may show books, illustrations, and terms and vocabulary they found to add to the classroom jazz word list. Students should be encouraged to teach the class about their musician. Thus, part 1 is an overview of the artist as well as an opportunity to place this artist in history, style, and jazz era.

TABLE F.4. Biography Selections

Armstrong, Louis
    Hacker, C. (1997). *Great African-Americans in jazz*. New York: Crabtree.
    Orgill, R. (1997). *If I only had a horn: Young Louis Armstrong*. Boston: Houghton Mifflin
    Schroeder, A. (1996). *Satchmo's blues*. New York: Doubleday.

Ellington, Duke
    Hacker, C. (1997). *Great African-Americans in jazz*. New York: Crabtree.
    Mour, S. I. (1998). *American jazz musicians*. Berkeley Heights, NJ: Enslow.
    Pinkney, A. D. (1998). *Duke Ellington: The piano prince and his orchestra*. New York: Hyperion Books.
    Venezia, M. (1995). *Duke Ellington*. Chicago: Children's Press.

Goodman, Benny
    Gourse, L. (1999). *Striders to beboppers and beyond: The art of jazz piano*. New York: Franklin Watts.
    Mour, S. I. (1998). *American jazz musicians*. Berkeley Heights, NJ: Enslow.
    Winter, J. (2000). *Once upon a time in Chicago: The story of Benny Goodman*. New York: Hyperion.

Marsalis, Wynton
    Gourse, L. (1999). *Striders to beboppers and beyond: The art of jazz piano*. New York: Franklin Watts.
    Hacker, C. (1997). *Great African-Americans in jazz*. New York: Crabtree.
    Mour, S. I. (1998). *American jazz musicians*. Berkeley Heights, NJ: Enslow.

Parker, Charlie
    Hacker, C. (1997). *Great African-Americans in jazz*. New York: Crabtree.
    Mour, S. I. (1998). *American jazz musicians*. Berkeley Heights, NJ: Enslow.
    Raschka, C. (1992). *Charlie Parker played bebop*. New York: Orchard.

Smith, Bessie
    Campbell, H. (1998). *Turnip blues*. New York: Spinsters Ink.
    Grifalconi, A. (1999). *Tiny's hat*. New York: HarperCollins
    Hacker, C. (1997). *Great African-Americans in jazz*. New York: Crabtree.

Williams, Mary Lou
    Dahl, L. (2000). *Morning glory: A biography of Mary Lou Williams*. New York: Pantheon.
    Gourse, L. (1999). *Striders to beboppers and beyond: The art of jazz piano*. New York: Franklin Watts.
    Mour, S. I. (1998). *American jazz musicians*. Berkeley Heights, NJ: Enslow.

Part 2: Listen to Our Artist

From an assortment provided by the teacher, the group selects a favorite recording of their artist (see Table F.1). This selection should typify the artist, style, and era in which the music was created. The presenter for this part should lead the whole class using the Listening to Jazz Checklist as a discovery activity about the recorded music of this artist. The group may choose to use an overhead or poster format as they lead this activity and discussion with the whole class.

Part 3: Our Artist in History

In the third part of the group presentation, students will place information they learned about their artist and music on the classroom jazz timeline. Contributions may include student illustrations, quotes from the artists, titles, musical descriptions, characteristics of key works, events and places of interest, and other information about the artist and the era in which the artist lived.

Part 4: Meet Our Artist

The final part of the group presentation involves a conversation with the artist. One or more members of the group become the actual musician featured in their biographical study. This character may be in costume and may hold or have drawn a representation of his/her instrument(s). The group may also create scenery as visual environment for the character. The character can tell a story about his or her life and music-making experiences. Following this introduction to the artist, the group invites the whole class to ask questions of the character while the panel assists as needed with the answers. Depending on the class composition, it might be helpful if the teacher prompts students with appropriate kinds of questions to ask to unveil the character.

TABLE F.5. Additional Resources for Teaching about Jazz

Blum, S. (Ed.). (1981). *Everyday fashions of the twenties.* New York: Dover Publications.

Brown, C. (1989). *The jazz experience.* New York: Brown.

Collier, J. (1991). *Duke Ellington.* New York: Macmillan.

Driggs, F., & Lewine, H. (1995). *Black beauty, white heat: A pictorial history of classic jazz, 1920–1950.* New York: Da Capo Press.

Edey, M. (Ed.). (1969). *This fabulous century* (Vols. 1–4). New York: Time-Life Books.

Gridley, M. (1997). *Jazz styles: History and analysis* (6th ed.). New York: Prentice Hall.

Gridley, M. (1997). *Concise guide to jazz* (3rd ed.). New York: Prentice Hall.

Haskins, J. (1997). *The cotton club.* New York: New American Library.

Kaplin, M., & Miers, C. (Eds.). (1987). *Harlem renaissance: Art of black America.* New York: The Studio Museum in Harlem.

Megill, D., & Demory, R. (2001). *Introduction to jazz history* (5th ed.). New York: Prentice Hall

Monceaux, M. (1994). *Jazz: My music, my people.* New York: Knopf.

Tirro, F. (1996). *Living with jazz: An appreciation.* New York: Harcourt Brace.

Event 5

As an outgrowth of the student presentations and as a way to assess student mastery of the standards, the final event in this Introduction to Jazz unit is a formal assessment of students' knowledge using the Listening to Jazz Checklist. Students are now familiar with the terms on the checklist and should be able correctly to identify musical characteristics as well as successfully identify various jazz recordings by era, style, and artist(s).

It seems reasonable that this final assessment contain several listening samples to stretch the students' ability to apply their listening and analytical skills to new listening media. Teachers may also want to include samples within this assessment that are not jazz (e.g., country western, classical, world music, etc.) to create contrast and challenge the students to analyze unknown samples of recorded music.

CONCLUSION

Our artistic respect for the groundbreaking creative energy and courage of past and present jazz artists drives us to seek out and experiment with (much like the improvisational nature of the artform itself) innovative ways to engage young students effectively and actively in creative and purposeful musical listening activities. Through the creative instructional pairing of quality children's literature about jazz with appropriate and authentic listening sample activities, our classrooms can easily serve to educate a whole new generation to love this important American art form. May the stories of jazz live on!

REFERENCES

Fisher, D., McDonald, N., & Strickland, J. (2001). Early literacy development: A sound practice. *General Music Today, 14*(3), 15–20.

Gollub, M. (2000). *The jazz fly*. Santa Rosa, CA: Tortuga Press.

Igus, T. (1998). *I see the rhythm*. San Francisco: Children's Book Press.

Moyers, S. (2000). Reading and writing workshop: Focus on biography. *Instructor, 109*(6), 61–64.

Music Educators National Conference. (1994). *The school music program: A new vision: The K–12 national standards, pre-K standards, and what they mean to music educators*. Reston, VA: Author.

Weatherford, C. (2000). *The sound that jazz makes*. New York: Walter and Company.

INDEX

Note: Page numbers followed by *f* refer to figures; those followed by *t* refer to tables.